A BASIC GUIDE TO
PATTERN DRAFTING

Volume 1

TORSO BLOCKS
SKIRTS
COLLARS
FACINGS
SLEEVES

NICK VERREOS
DAVID PAUL

Welcome to the World of Pattern Drafting!

Patternmaking for fashion design is comprised of creating paper templates of a garment that are then cut in fabric and subsequently sewn. It is an essential and vital step in the design and creation of clothing.

This handbook is to be used as a supplemental guide in addition to the traditional textbook provided by your school. Think of it as a "Quick Guide", giving the student of patternmaking an additional tool to help them understand the basic principles of patternmaking.

From Blocks to the basics of dresses, skirts, tops, sleeves and collars, this will provide you the extra assistance you need to understand the fundamentals of patternmaking.

As an instructor of patternmaking with over 25 years of professional experience in the fashion industry, I have compiled this book as a means to support and aid beginners in their quest to become proficient in patternmaking and understand how integral it is to Fashion Design.

BIOGRAPHY

Nick and David co-founded NIKOLAKI, in 2001. Their collections of upscale red carpet gowns and cocktail dresses have been worn by celebrities such as Beyoncé, Katy Perry, Heidi Klum, Eva Longoria and Carrie Underwood. NIKOLAKI has been carried in over 100 stores across the US and abroad.

Additionally, they design and produce NV Nick Verreos a clothing line which is available on major Home Shopping Networks including Evine Live (USA), QVC UK, QVC Italy and The Shopping Channel (Canada).

Nick was the Winning Mentor of Project Runway: Under the Gunn and first received national and international attention after appearing on Project Runway. He is a red carpet fashion expert and correspondent for various networks including E! Entertainment and ABC's "On The Red Carpet" LIVE from the Oscars.

Nick Received his Bachelor of Arts in Political Science at the University of California, Los Angeles/UCLA. He then continued on to the Fashion Institute of Design & Merchandising/FIDM, where he graduated from the Advanced Fashion Design Program.

As an educator, Nick has been an instructor at FIDM where he taught Fashion Sketching, Draping, Patternmaking and Design.

A native of Southern California, David Paul Attended the University of California, Los Angeles/UCLA where he received his Bachelor of Arts in Theatre Arts and subsequently, his MFA in Costume Design.

David went on to build an extensive resume in the world of entertainment and fashion styling for over 20 years. As a member of IATSE Local 705, David designed costumes and worked on shows such as "Queer Eye for the Straight Girl", "Passions", "Undressed" and numerous other productions for MTV, ABC, FOX, NIKELODEON and the WB.

David has also worked alongside Andre Leon Talley and Lisa Love for Vogue Magazine and with such illustrious photographers as Arthur Elgort, Regan Cameron, Noe DeWitt and Amanda DeCadanet, styling for Kate Hudson, Heidi Klum, Vanessa Paradis, Twiggy and Heather Graham.

Nick and David are Co-Chairs of Fashion Design, Advanced Fashion Design, Advanced Theatre Costume, Film & TV Costume, Jewelry and Footwear at the Fashion Institute of Design & Merchandising/FIDM. They also co-authored the best-selling book, A Passion for Fashion, which was the #1 New Release on Amazon for Fashion and Textile Business.

TABLE OF CONTENTS

SKIRTS

SLEEVES

NOTCHES

-Notches are small marks made on the pattern to ensure that one pattern piece will match up to it's adjoining pattern.
-They can be used to show what the value of the seam allowance is, and can also be used as markers along a seam to make sure that the two pieces of fabric will come together correctly when sewn.
-Sometimes they can also be defined as "Sew me to Sew me" marks.

GUIDE TO WHERE TO NOTCH on Basic Drapes/Patterns:
A) Shoulder:

B) Side Seams:

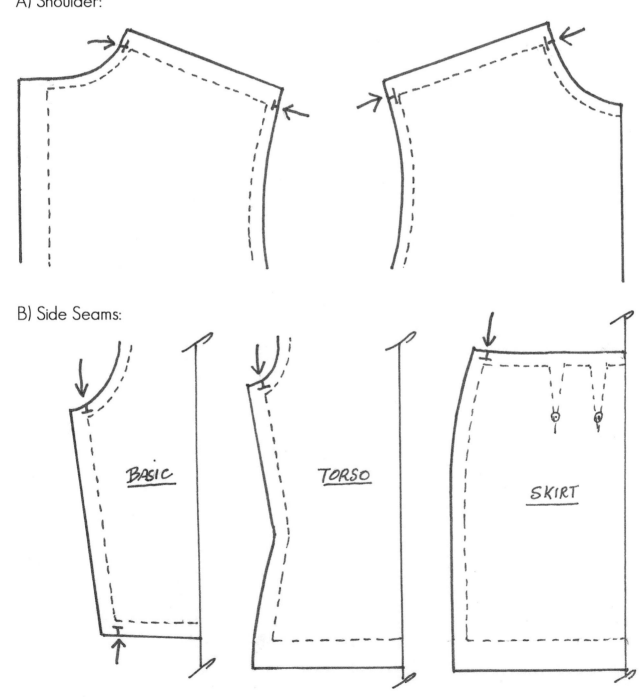

BASIC

TORSO

SKIRT

NOTCHES

C) Center Front—On the FOLD and CF with opening:

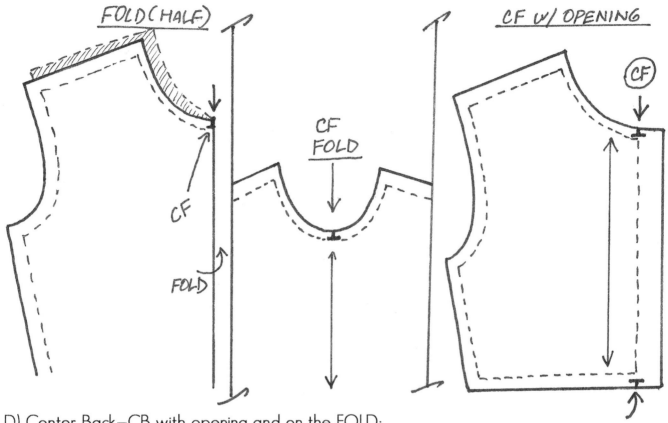

FOLD (HALF)

CF

FOLD

CF FOLD

CF w/ OPENING

CF

D) Center Back—CB with opening and on the FOLD:

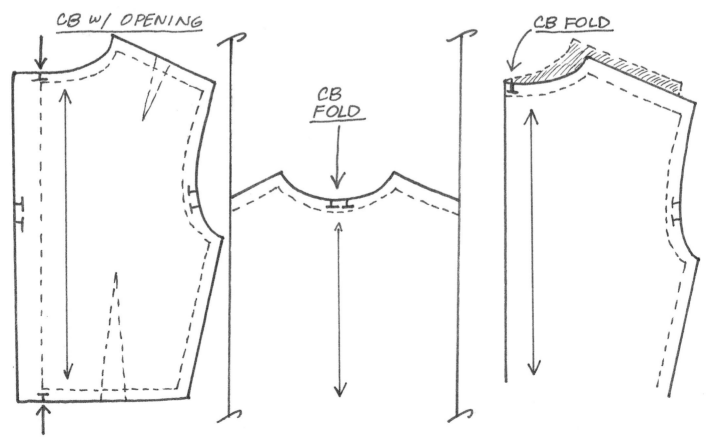

CB w/ OPENING

CB FOLD

CB FOLD

NOTCHES

NO's of Notching:

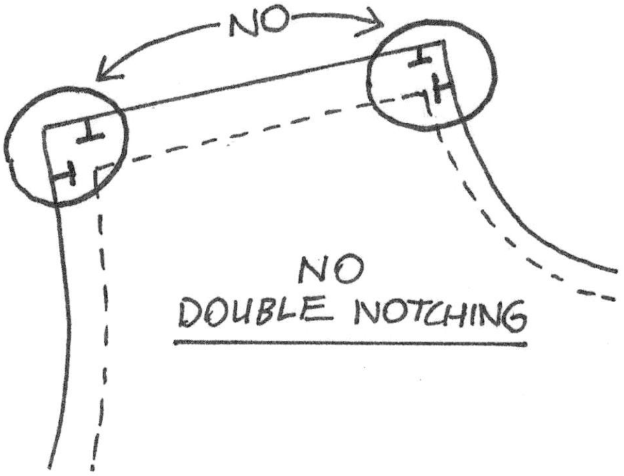

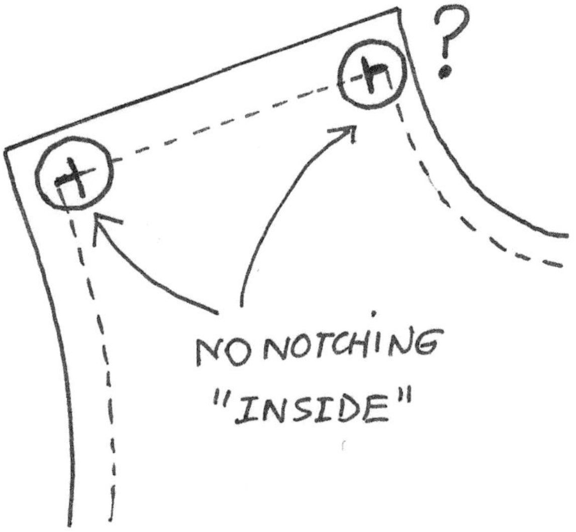

YES's of Notching:

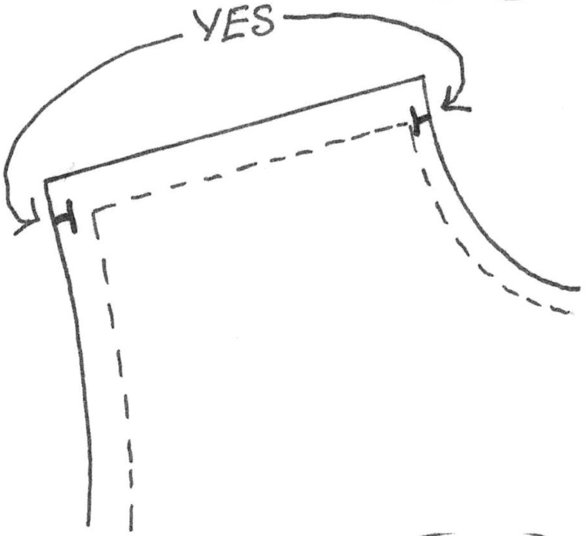

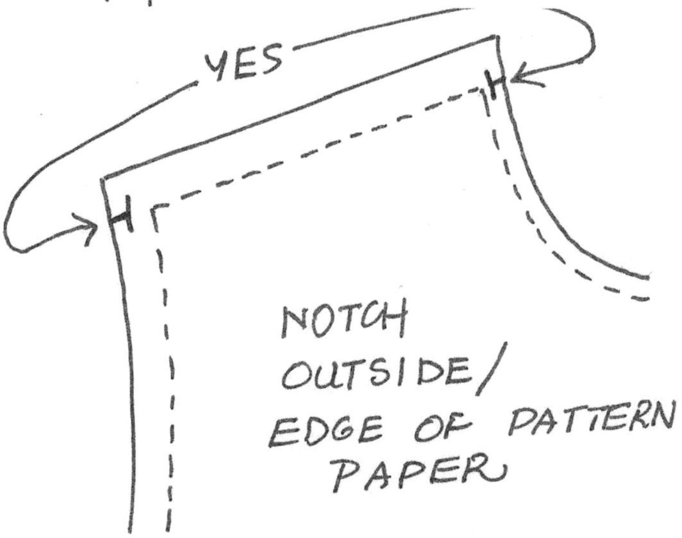

YES

NO

NO DOUBLE NOTCHING

?

NO NOTCHING "INSIDE"

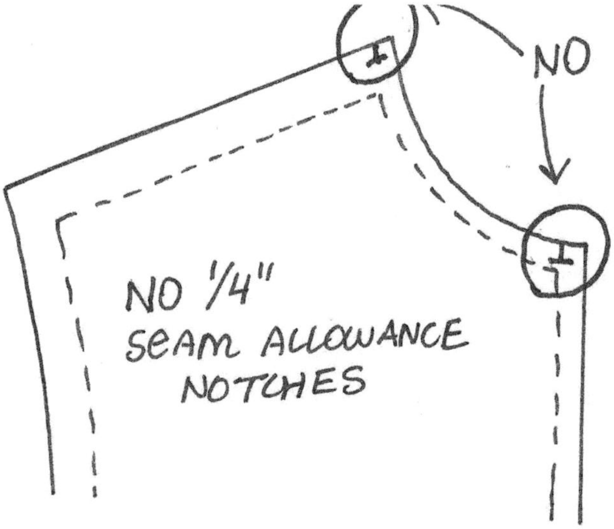

YES

NOTCH OUTSIDE/ EDGE OF PATTERN PAPER

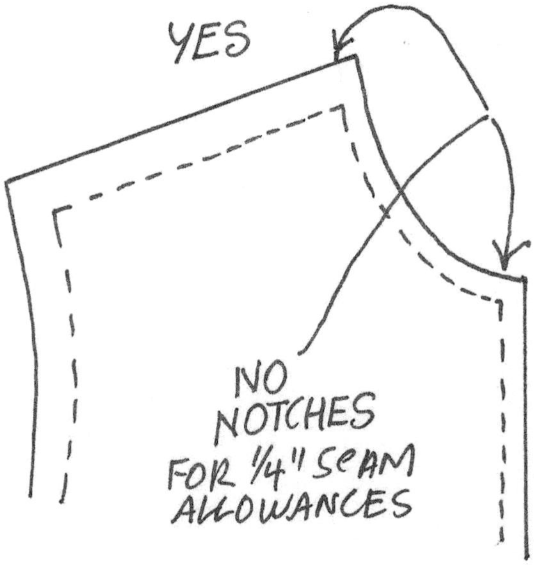

NO

NO 1/4" SEAM ALLOWANCE NOTCHES

YES

NO NOTCHES FOR 1/4" SEAM ALLOWANCES

BLOCKS/SLOPERS
BASIC DRESS

-A Block (or sloper) is a simple master pattern used to make more detailed patterns. Blocks generally have no design features and therefore are a basic foundation for more complicated patterns.

-Before cutting and sewing your basic dress, made from your blocks, add correct seam allowance and appropriate notches:

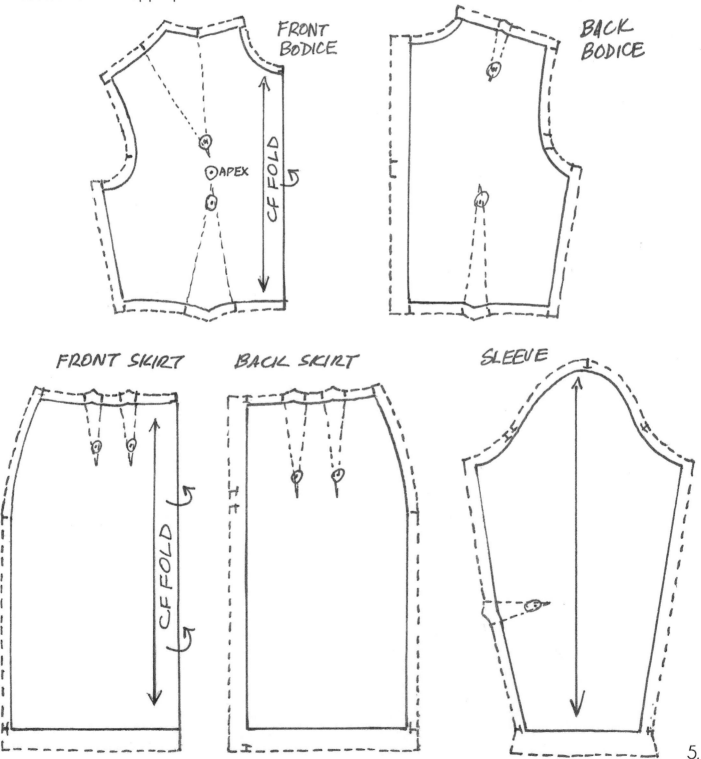

FRONT BODICE

APEX

CF FOLD

BACK BODICE

FRONT SKIRT

CF FOLD

BACK SKIRT

SLEEVE

MARKER
BASIC DRESS

-Markers are a guide used in the cutting process. It is usually a long sheet of paper with all the pattern pieces positioned in a configuration intended to reduce fabric waist.

-Lay out your patterns on marker paper to ensure the least amount of waste. After deciding the position of each pattern piece, trace outlines of each pattern on the marker paper.

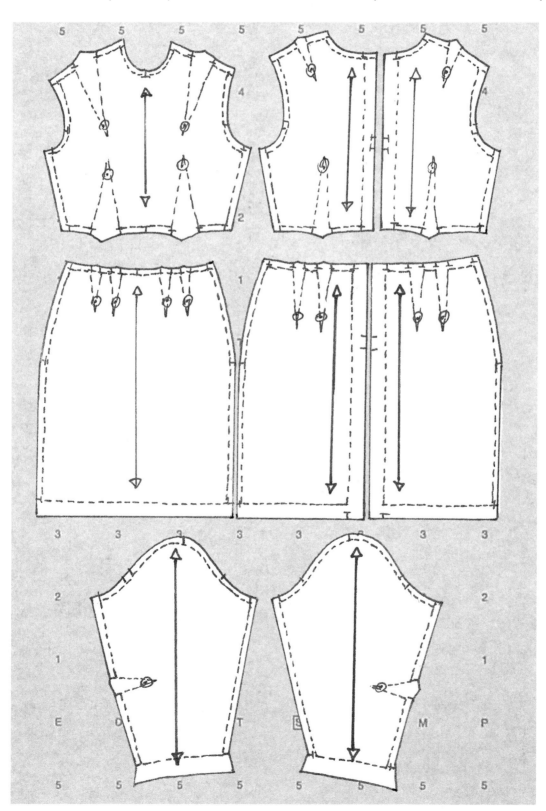

1-DART SLOPER:
-Use 2-Dart Basic Sloper to create 1-Dart Sloper.

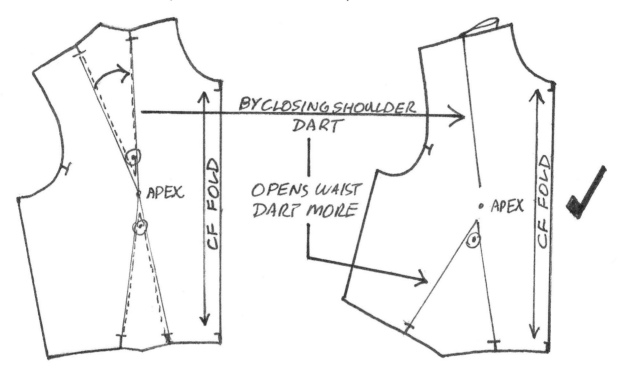

BY CLOSING SHOULDER DART

OPENS WAIST DART MORE

APEX

CF FOLD

APEX

CF FOLD

2-DART SLOPER #2: Side Bust and Waist Darts:
-Use 1-Dart Sloper to create this 2-Dart Sloper #2.

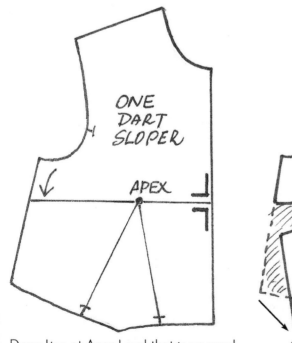

ONE DART SLOPER

APEX

Draw Line at Apex Level that is squared to the center front

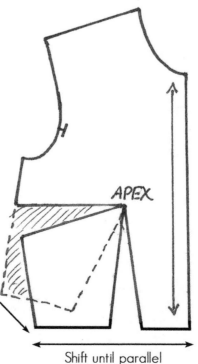

APEX

Shift until parallel

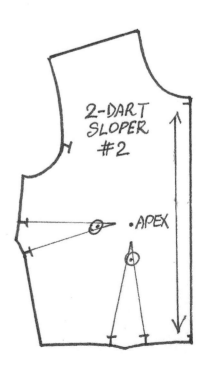

2-DART SLOPER #2

APEX

DARTS

DART ELIMINATION: PRINCESS LINE

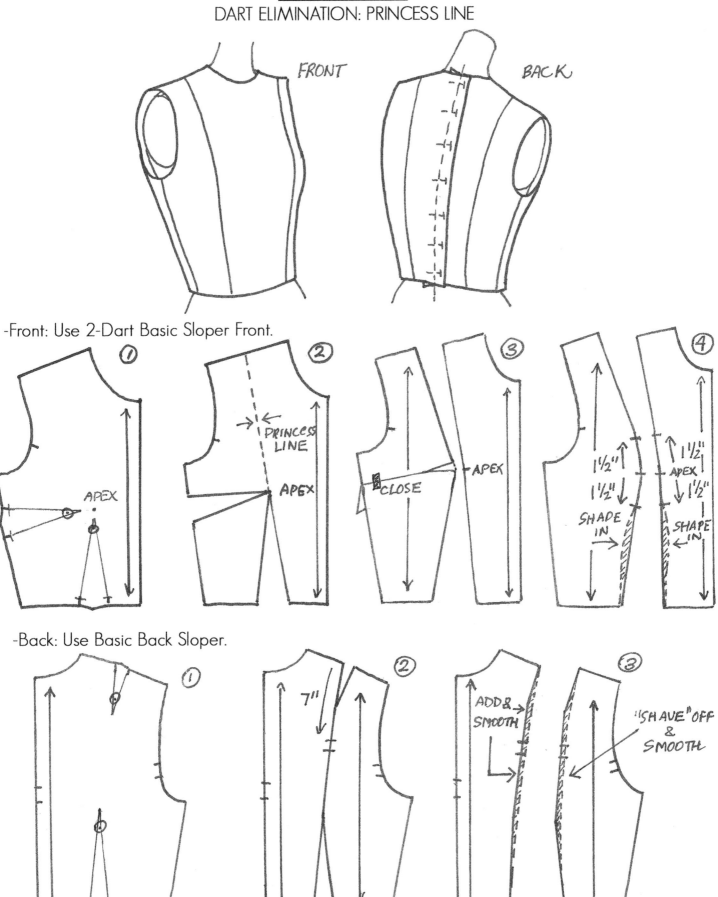

FRONT

BACK

-Front: Use 2-Dart Basic Sloper Front.

① APEX

② PRINCESS LINE · APEX

③ CLOSE · APEX

④ 1½" · 1½" · SHADE IN · 1½" · APEX · 1½" · SHAPE IN

-Back: Use Basic Back Sloper.

①

② 7"

③ ADD & SMOOTH · "SHAVE" OFF & SMOOTH

8.

DARTS
TRANSFERING AND ELIMINATION

YOKE AND SHIRRING:

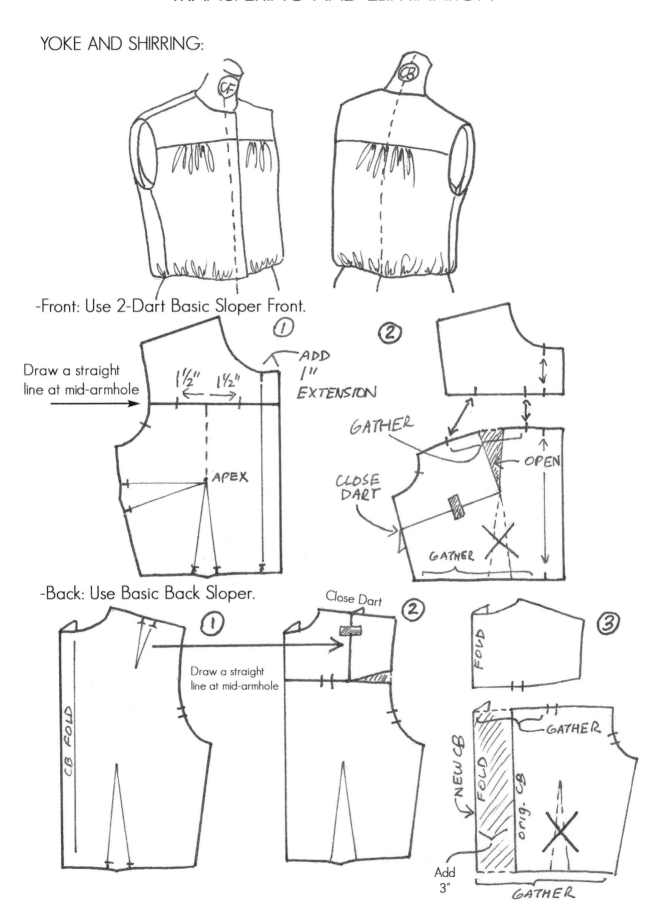

-Front: Use 2-Dart Basic Sloper Front.

① ②

ADD 1" EXTENSION

Draw a straight line at mid-armhole →

1½" 1½"

APEX

GATHER

CLOSE DART

OPEN

GATHER

-Back: Use Basic Back Sloper.

Close Dart

① ②

Draw a straight line at mid-armhole →

CB FOLD

③

FOLD

NEW CB FOLD

orig. CB

GATHER

Add 3"

GATHER

BASIC DRESS

-The Basic Dress is the foundation garment for introductory pattern making. On the following pages you will find instructions on how to sewing this dress.

Basic Dress

SEWING INSTRUCTIONS

1) Start by cutting out all pattern pieces in muslin adding proper seam allowances including 1" center back seam allowance and 1" hem allowance.

2) Sew DARTS: When sewing darts, make sure to end 1/2" past drill/punch hole. Press FRONT DARTS toward FRONT. Press BACK DARTS toward BACK.

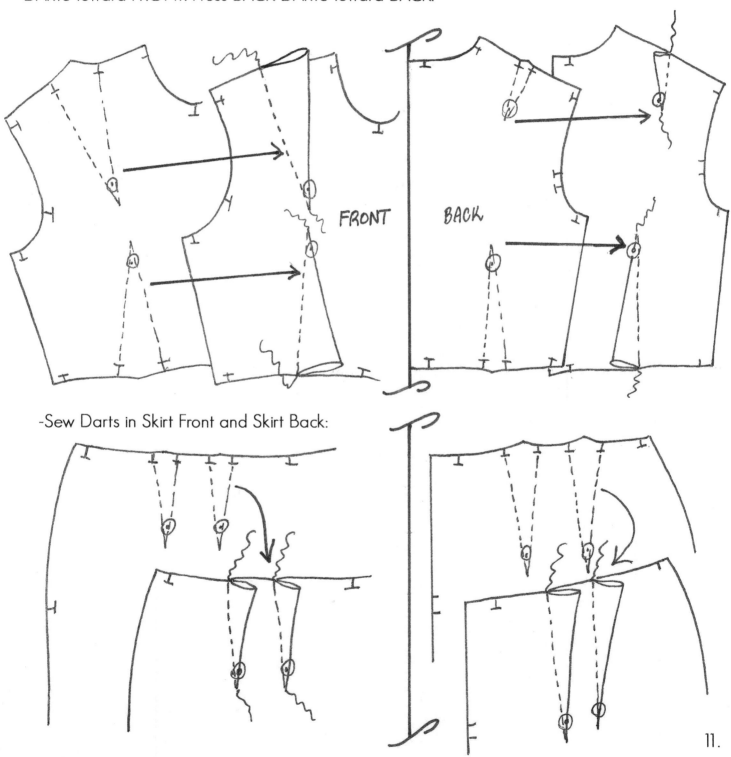

FRONT   BACK

-Sew Darts in Skirt Front and Skirt Back:

BASIC DRESS
SEWING INSTRUCTIONS

2) Sew SHOULDERS at 1/2" seam allowance. Make sure darts match, front to back. Press open.

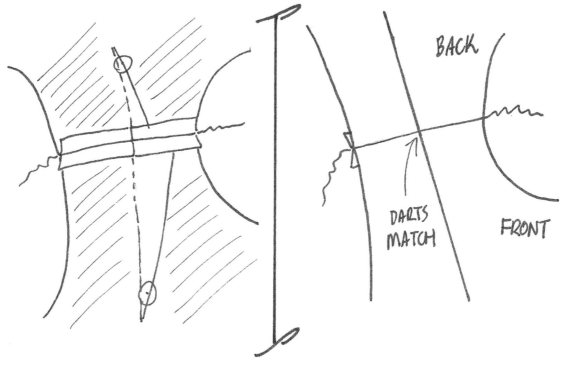

BACK

DARTS
MATCH

FRONT

3) Sew SIDE SEAMS of Bodice and Skirt sections at 1/2" seam allowance. Press open.

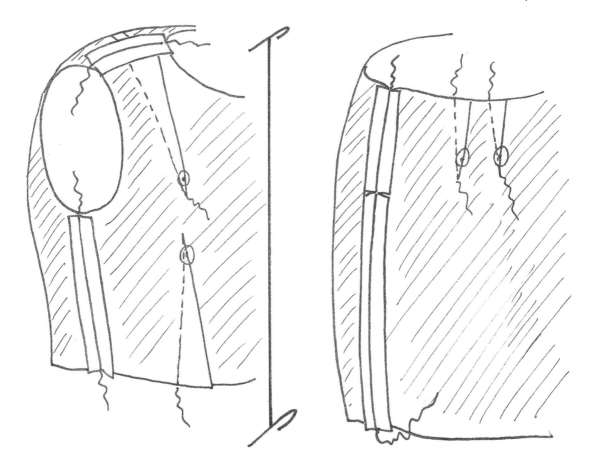

Basic Dress

SEWING INSTRUCTIONS

4) Sew WAIST at 1/2" seam allowance, putting together the BODICE with the SKIRT. Make sure SIDE SEAMS and DARTS match up. Press seams open (some sewers press waist seam up or down.) Refer to instructor for preferred method.

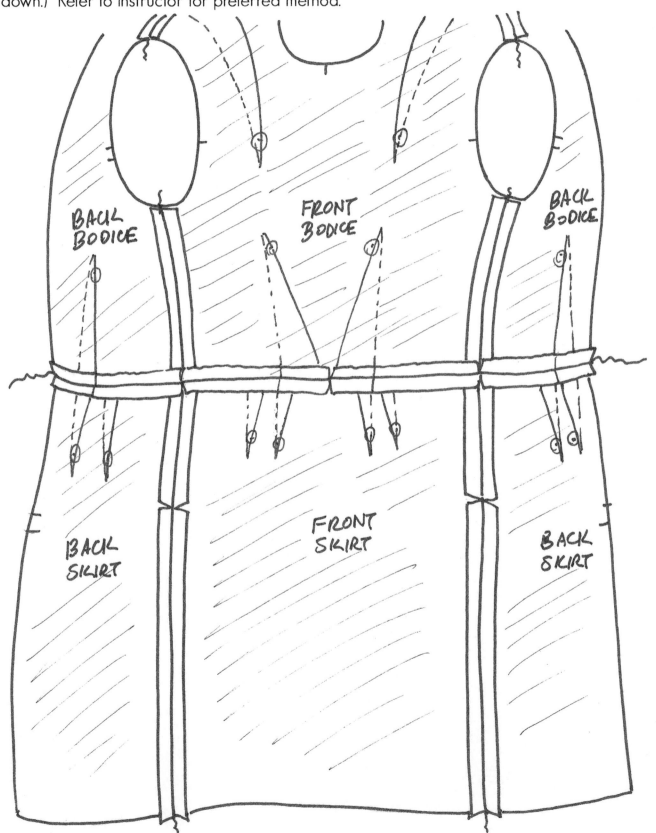

Basic Dress

5) Sew SLEEVES:
   Sew elbow DARTS on each sleeve. Remember to sew 1/2" past punch/drill hole.
   Press darts downward toward hem of sleeve.

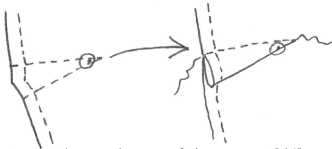

   -Sew 2 crimping/basting stitches on the cap of sleeve, one 1/4" away from cap edge and the other 5/8" away from cap edge. The stitches are from back notch to front notch. After sewing them, lightly pull them to create light crimping, but NOT gathering/shirring.

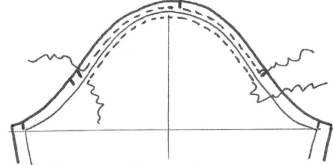

   -Sew underarm seam at 1/2" seam allowance. Press open.

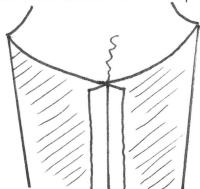

   -Sew SLEEVES onto bodice using 1/2" seam allowance. Press seam allowance toward sleeve as opposed to pressing toward the body of the dress.

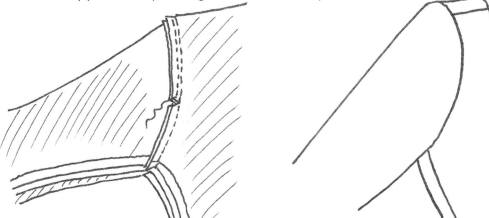

SEWING INSTRUCTIONS

6) Sew HEM of Sleeves at 1". Press.

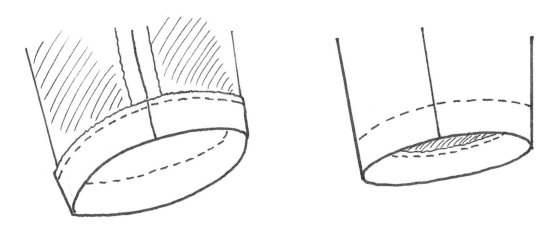

7) Sew HEM of Dress at 1". Press.

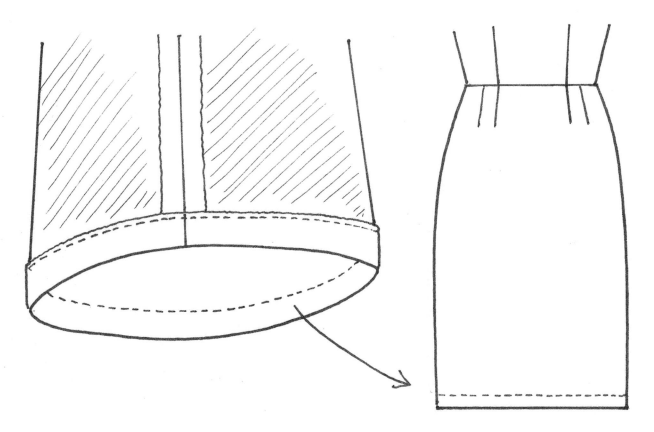

● Finish with overall pressing to make Dress presentable ●

TORSO
BLOCK/SLOPER

-On the following pages you will find instructions on how to draft the TORSO BLOCK seen below:

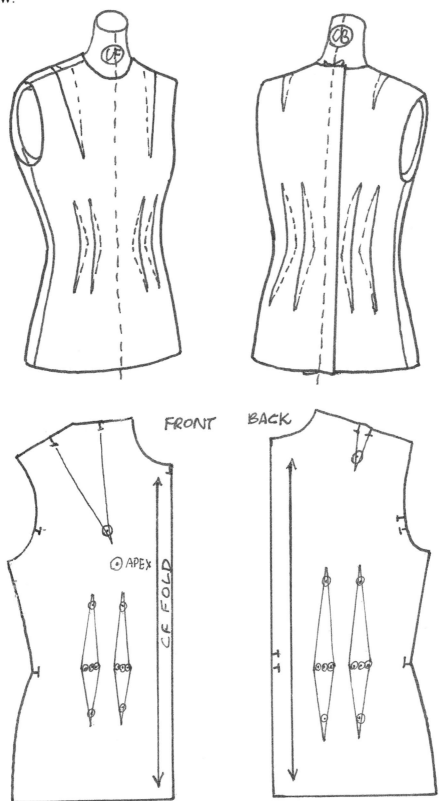

FRONT   BACK

APEX

CF FOLD

TORSO
BLOCK/SLOPER

Drafting the TORSO BLOCK:

-Use BASIC BODICE FRONT and BASIC BODICE BACK

FRONT TORSO:
-Draw a vertical line 30" long to represent the center front, Label (A).
-Square a line about 20" down from the top, Label (B).
-Square another line 8" down from (B) and label (C).
-Both (B) and (C) lines are 9 1/2" long.
-Place Basic Bodice Front as shown, making sure the Center Front aligns
 with line (A) and waist touches line (B).

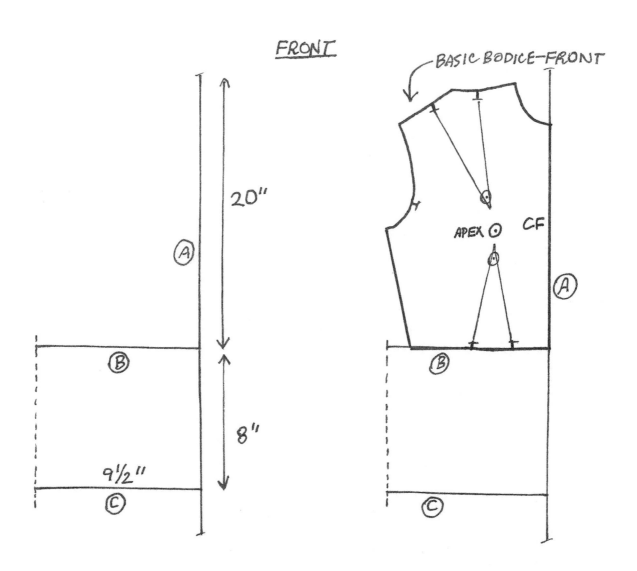

FRONT

TORSO
BLOCK/SLOPER

BACK TORSO:
-Draw a vertical line 30" long to represent the center back, Label (A).
-Square a line about 20" down from the top, Label (B).
-Square another line 8" down from (B) and label (C).
-Both (B) and (C) lines are 10" long.
-Place Basic Bodice Back as shown, making sure the Center Back aligns with line (A) and waist touches line (B).

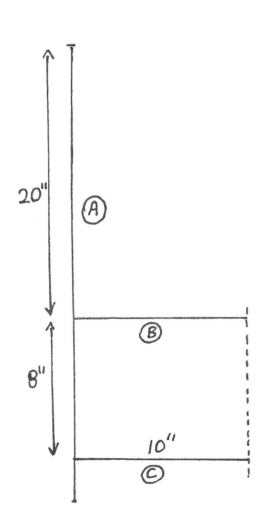

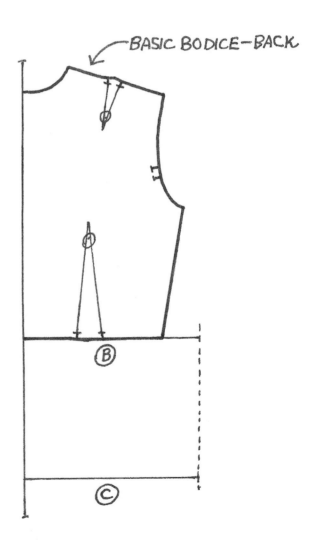

BASIC BODICE-BACK

SIDE SEAMS:

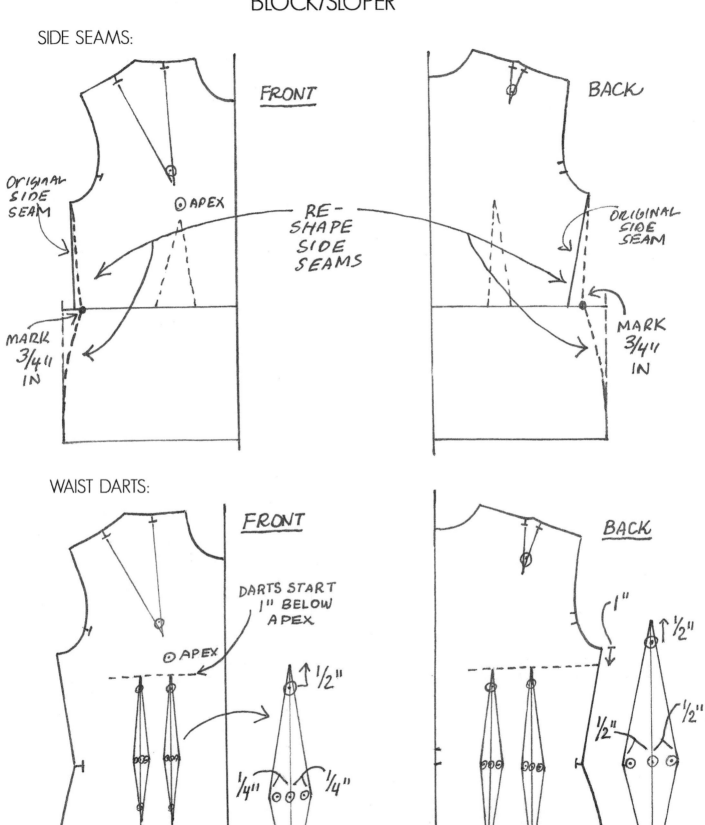

FRONT

BACK

ORIGINAL SIDE SEAM

ORIGINAL SIDE SEAM

⊙ APEX

RE-SHAPE SIDE SEAMS

MARK 3/4" IN

MARK 3/4" IN

WAIST DARTS:

FRONT

BACK

DARTS START 1" BELOW APEX

⊙ APEX

↑1/2"

↑1/2"

1/4" 1/4"

1/2"

1/2"

1 3/4"

2 1/4"

↓1/2"

1"

↓1/2"

19.

TORSO
BLOCK/SLOPER

-Make sure FRONT and BACK patterns are parallel at side seams, from WAIST down:

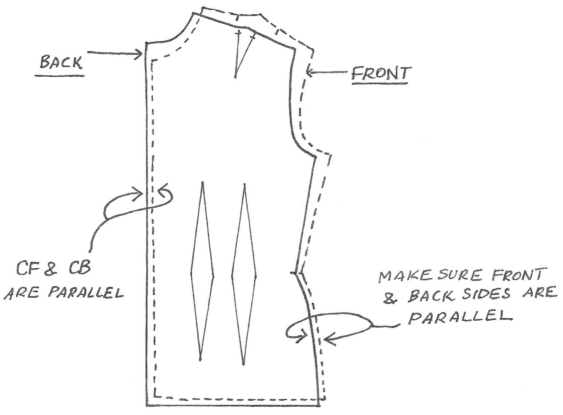

BACK → ← FRONT

CF & CB
ARE PARALLEL

MAKE SURE FRONT
& BACK SIDES ARE
PARALLEL

-Finish TORSO BLOCK patterns:

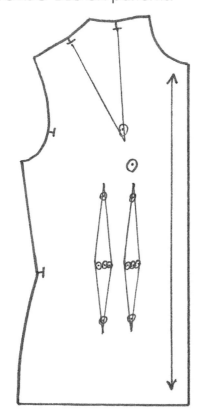
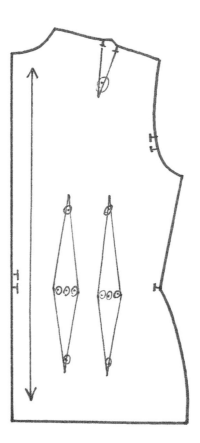

FACINGS

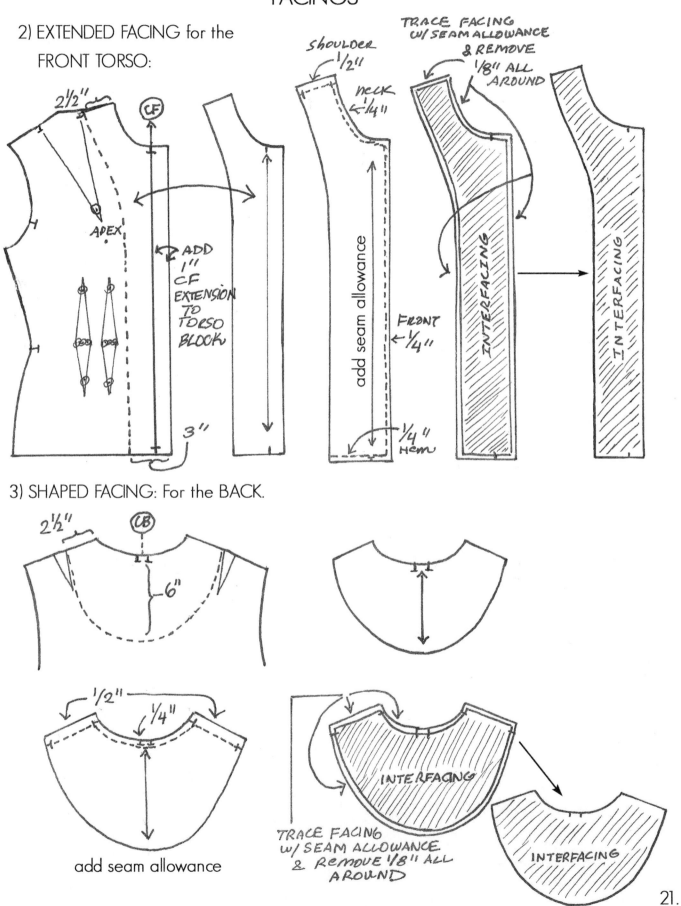

2) EXTENDED FACING for the FRONT TORSO:

2½"

CF

APEX

ADD 1" CF EXTENSION TO TORSO BLOCK

3"

TRACE FACING w/ SEAM ALLOWANCE & REMOVE ⅛" ALL AROUND

shoulder ½"

neck ¼"

add seam allowance

FRONT ¼"

¼" Hem

INTERFACING

INTERFACING

3) SHAPED FACING: For the BACK.

2½"

CB

6"

½"

¼"

add seam allowance

INTERFACING

TRACE FACING w/ SEAM ALLOWANCE & REMOVE ⅛" ALL AROUND

INTERFACING

TORSO
FACINGS

4) SHIRT PLACKET:

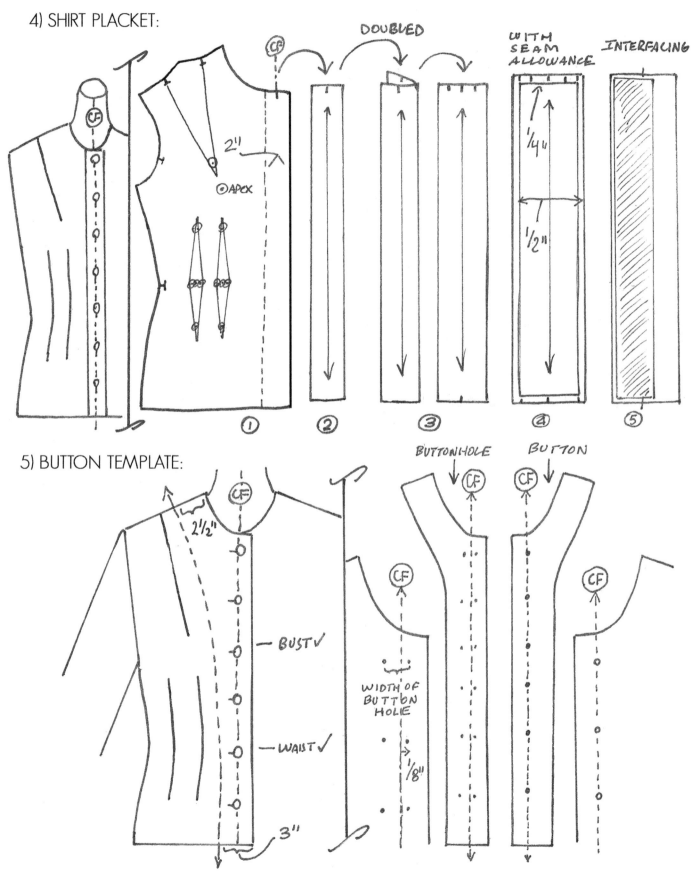

DOUBLED

WITH SEAM ALLOWANCE

INTERFACING

CF

2"

⊙APEX

1/4"

1/2"

① ② ③ ④ ⑤

5) BUTTON TEMPLATE:

BUTTONHOLE   BUTTON

CF

CF

CF

CF

2 1/2"

BUST ✓

WAIST ✓

WIDTH OF BUTTON HOLE

1/8"

3"

TORSO
BLOCK/SLOPER
SEWING INSTRUCTIONS

1) Add Seam Allowance to Front and Back Torso Sloper Block; then cut Front and Back Torso Sloper Block in muslin:

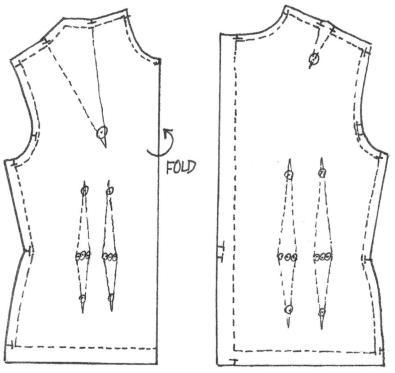

2) Sew Darts:
   - Sew Shoulder Darts. Press Front Shoulder Darts toward CENTER FRONT; press Back Shoulder Darts toward CENTER BACK:

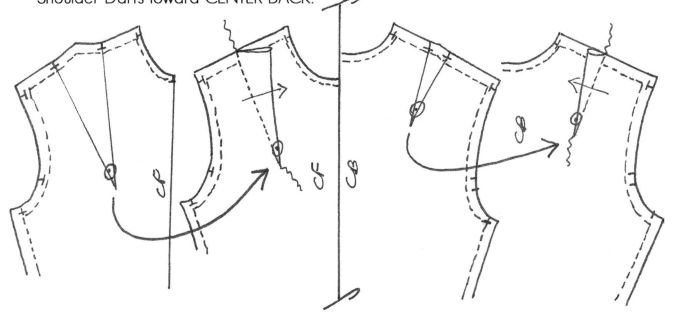

TORSO
BLOCK/SLOPER
SEWING INSTRUCTIONS

-Sew Front and Back Waist "fisheye" Darts. Press Front Waist Fisheye Darts toward the CENTER FRONT; press the Back Waist Fisheye Darts toward the CENTER BACK:

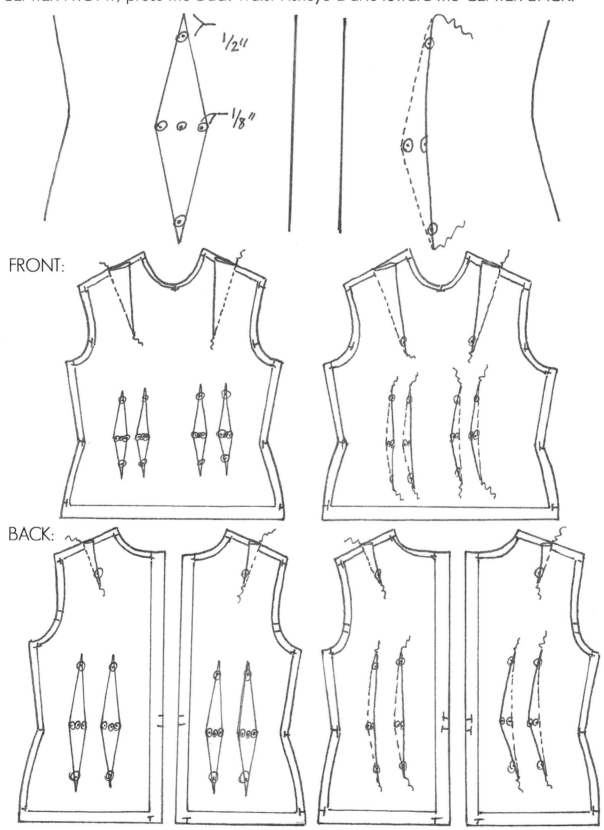

FRONT:

BACK:

24.

TORSO
BLOCK/SLOPER
SEWING INSTRUCTIONS

3)Sew Shoulder Seams; press open:

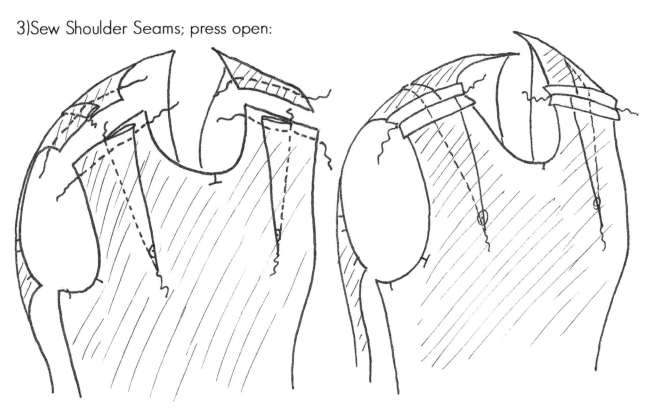

4)Sew Side Seams; press open:

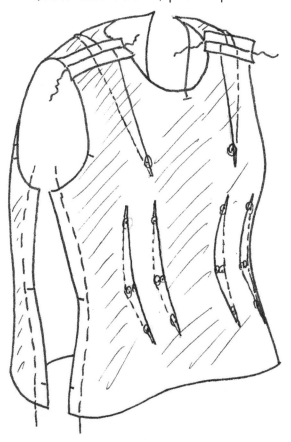
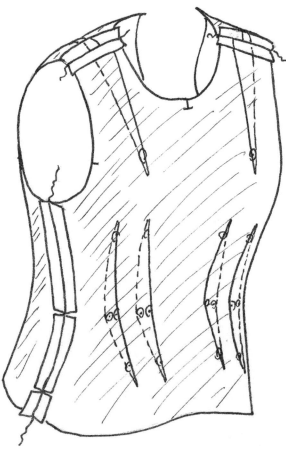

5)Sew Hem. Turn the Hem 1" and press:

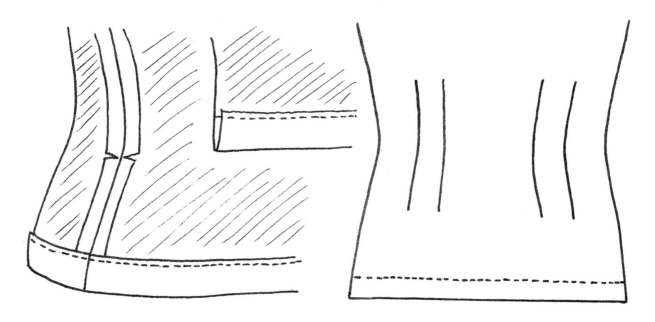

6)Staystitch the neckline 1/4":

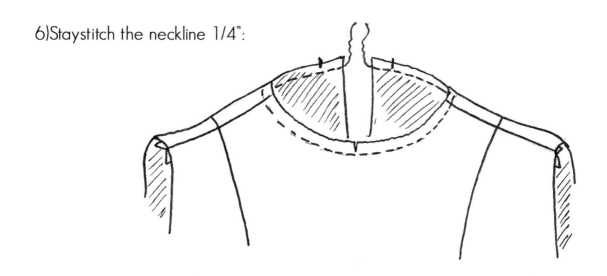

COLLARS

CONVERTIBLE SHIRT COLLAR

**Always refer to Instructor's Demo and Textbook for more detailed instructions on drafting COLLARS.

-Top Collar:

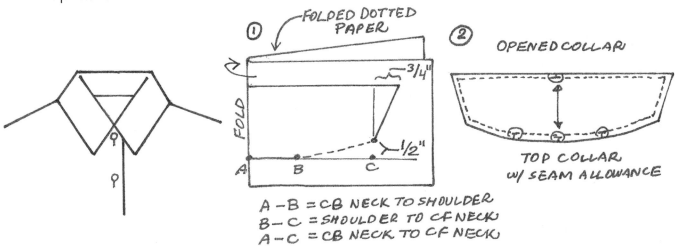

① FOLDED DOTTED PAPER
~3/4"
FOLD
1/2"
A   B   C
② OPENED COLLAR
TOP COLLAR w/ SEAM ALLOWANCE

A – B = CB NECK TO SHOULDER
B – C = SHOULDER TO CF NECK
A – C = CB NECK TO CF NECK

-Undercollar:

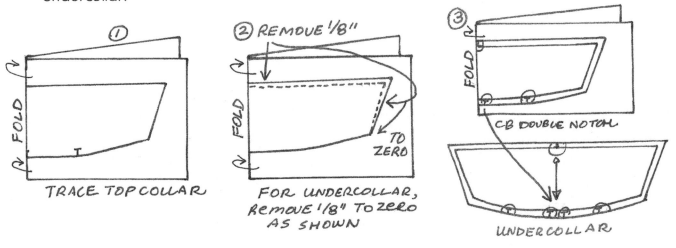

① FOLD — TRACE TOP COLLAR

② REMOVE 1/8" — FOLD — TO ZERO — FOR UNDERCOLLAR, REMOVE 1/8" TO ZERO AS SHOWN

③ FOLD — CB DOUBLE NOTCH — UNDERCOLLAR

-Top Collar Interfacing:

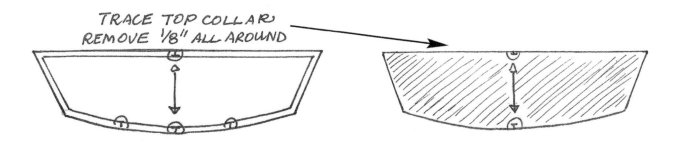

TRACE TOP COLLAR REMOVE 1/8" ALL AROUND

COLLARS
MANDARIN COLLAR

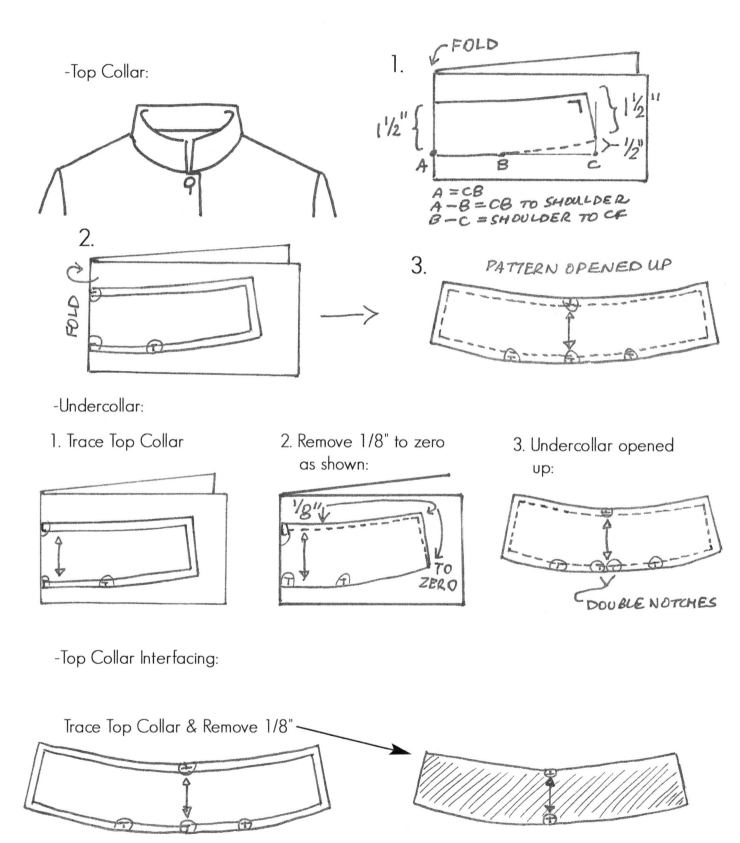

-Top Collar:

1. FOLD

1½" 1½"
½"
A   B   C

A = CB
A-B = CB TO SHOULDER
B-C = SHOULDER TO CF

2. FOLD

3. PATTERN OPENED UP

-Undercollar:

1. Trace Top Collar

2. Remove 1/8" to zero as shown:
1/8"
TO ZERO

3. Undercollar opened up:
DOUBLE NOTCHES

-Top Collar Interfacing:

Trace Top Collar & Remove 1/8"

PETER PAN COLLAR

Use ONE DART SLOPER Front and BASIC BODICE BACK SLOPER to draft

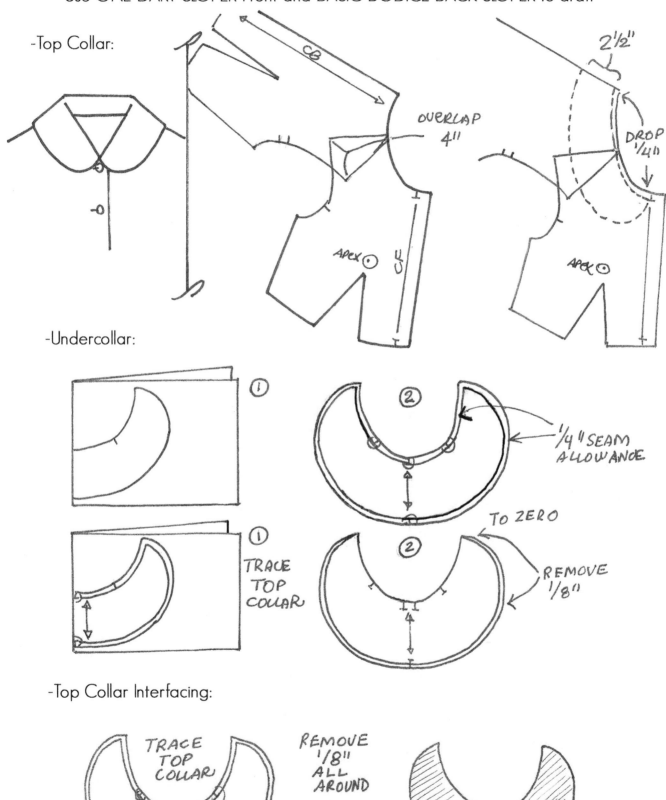

-Top Collar:

CB

OVERLAP 4"

APEX ⊙

CF

2½"

DROP ¼"

APEX ⊙

-Undercollar:

①

②

¼" SEAM ALLOWANCE

①

TRACE TOP COLLAR

②

TO ZERO

REMOVE ⅛"

-Top Collar Interfacing:

TRACE TOP COLLAR

REMOVE ⅛" ALL AROUND

SKIRTS
A-LINE SKIRT

-Use 2-Dart Skirt Block to draft A-Line Skirt

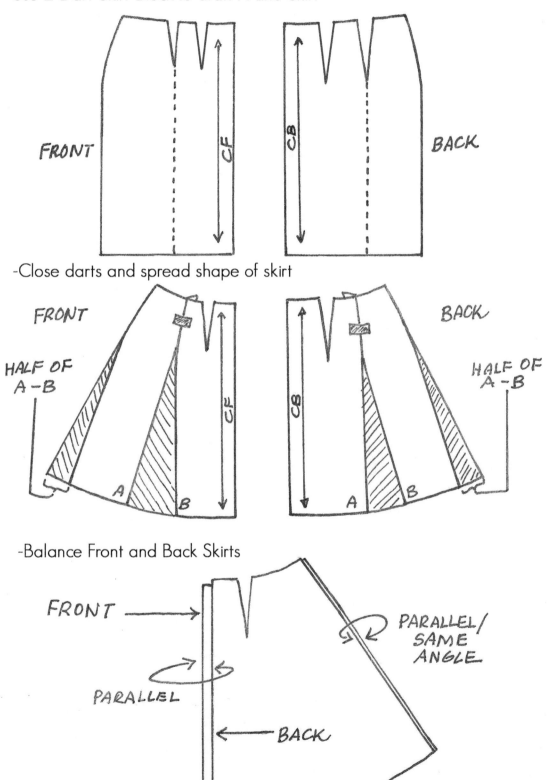

FRONT   CF   CB   BACK

-Close darts and spread shape of skirt

FRONT   BACK

HALF OF
A – B

HALF OF
A – B

CF   CB

A   B   A   B

-Balance Front and Back Skirts

FRONT

PARALLEL/
SAME
ANGLE

PARALLEL

BACK

SKIRTS
6-GORE SKIRT

-A GORED SKIRT is a skirt that is divided into panels, or gores. Gored Skirts can contain various numbers of panels; from 4 to 12 or more. It is important that each joining panel must be notched to ensure the correct gore matches the corresponding gore. A 6-GORE SKIRT is one of the most popular designs among the paneled skirts. It is comprised of 3 panels in the front and 3 in the back:

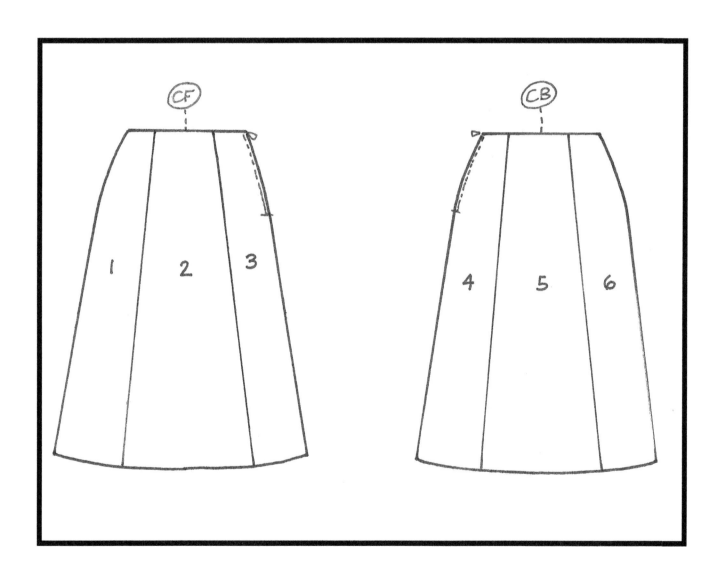

SKIRTS
6-GORE SKIRT

-Drafting A 6-GORE SKIRT:

    A) Use the Basic 2-DART Skirt Block/Sloper:

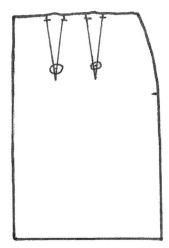 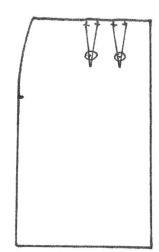

    B) MODIFY DARTS:

      -Take the amount of DART #2 and ADD IT to DART #1 as shown.
      Do this for both FRONT and BACK:

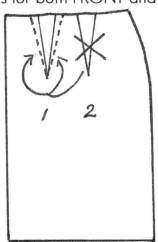 

-Final MODIFIED Skirt:

 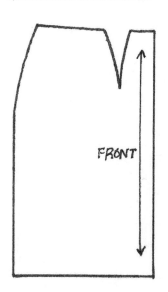

BACK   FRONT

SKIRTS
6-GORE SKIRT

C) Mark GORE SECTIONS:

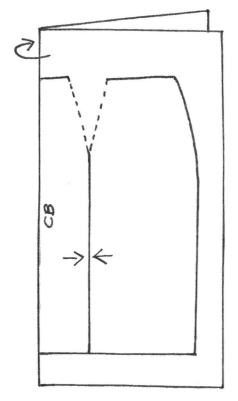
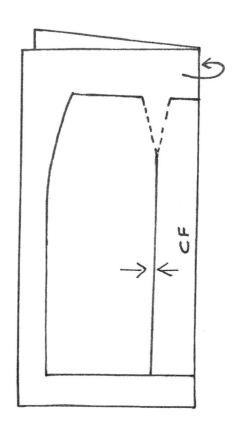

D) Add 2" at each side of GORE SECTIONS:

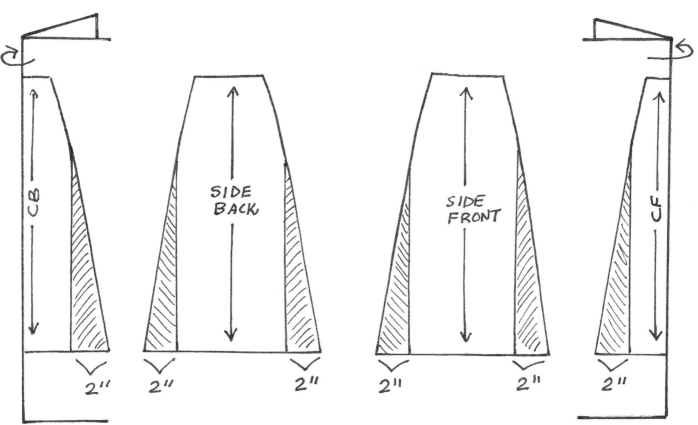

SKIRTS
6-GORE SKIRT

E) Square Sides at hem of GORE SECTIONS as shown:

BEFORE

SQUARED

BEFORE

SQUARED

SIDE BACK

② NOTCHES

SIDE BACK →

← SIDE

BACK

SIDE BACK

F) Add seam allowances and notches:

SIDE FRONT →

① NOTCH

C.F.

SIDE

SIDE FRONT

① NOTCH

SIDE FRONT

-Waist Facings for 6-Gore Skirt:

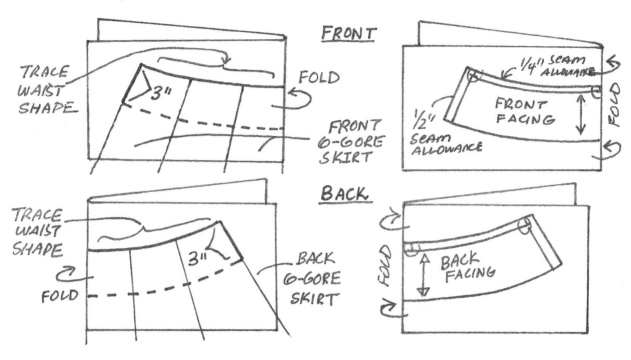

FRONT

TRACE WAIST SHAPE

3"

FOLD

FRONT 6-GORE SKIRT

1/4" SEAM ALLOWANCE

1/2" SEAM ALLOWANCE

FRONT FACING

FOLD

BACK

TRACE WAIST SHAPE

FOLD

3"

BACK 6-GORE SKIRT

FOLD

BACK FACING

-Waist Facings/Interfacing Patterns: Trace Facings and remove 1/8" all around:

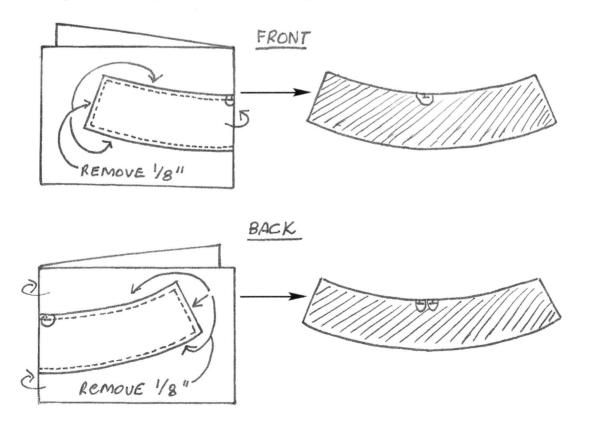

FRONT

REMOVE 1/8"

BACK

REMOVE 1/8"

HIP YOKE WITH FULLNESS SKIRT

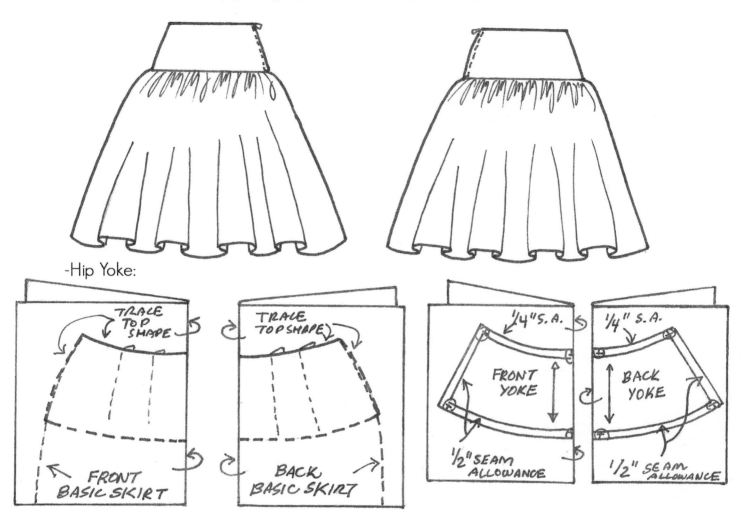

-Hip Yoke:

TRACE TOP SHAPE

FRONT BASIC SKIRT

TRACE TOP SHAPE

BACK BASIC SKIRT

1/4" S.A.

FRONT YOKE

1/2" SEAM ALLOWANCE

1/4" S.A.

BACK YOKE

1/2" SEAM ALLOWANCE

-Gathered Skirt/Skirt with Fullness:

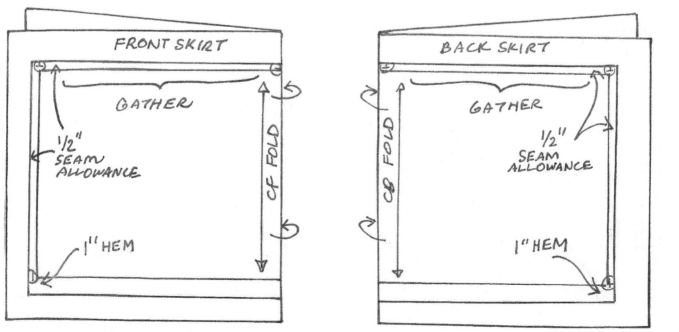

FRONT SKIRT

GATHER

1/2" SEAM ALLOWANCE

CF FOLD

1" HEM

BACK SKIRT

GATHER

CB FOLD

1/2" SEAM ALLOWANCE

1" HEM

A-LINE HIP YOKE WITH INVERTED CENTER FRONT PLEAT

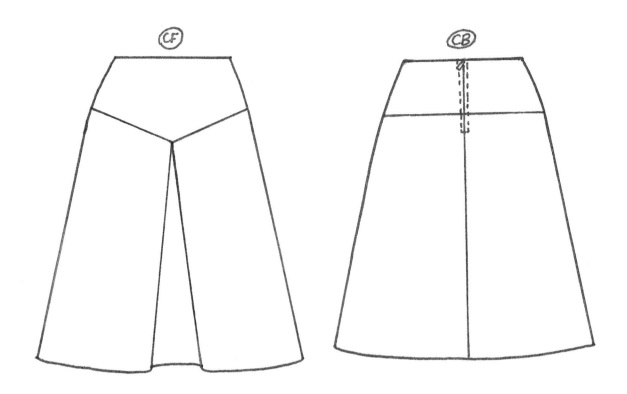

-Yoke Pattern:

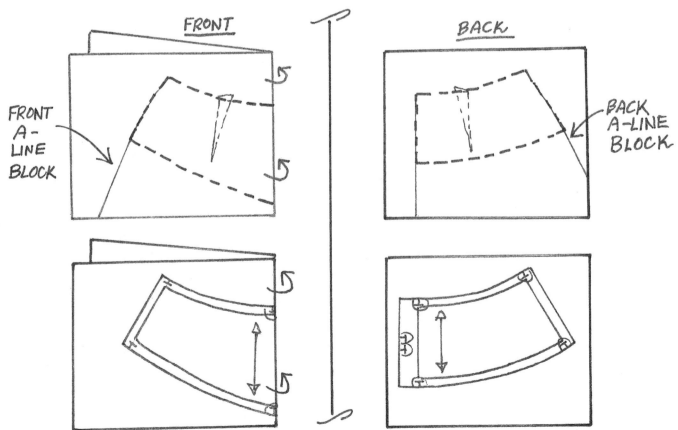

SKIRTS

A-LINE HIP YOKE WITH INVERTED CENTER FRONT PLEAT

-Adding the pleat to FRONT of A-Line Skirt pattern with Seam Allowance:

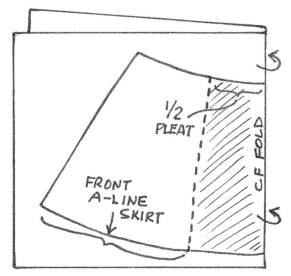

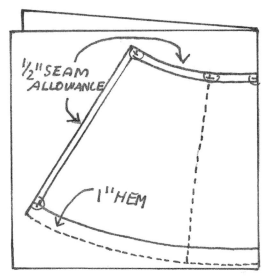

-Skirt section with CF Box Pleat OPENED UP:

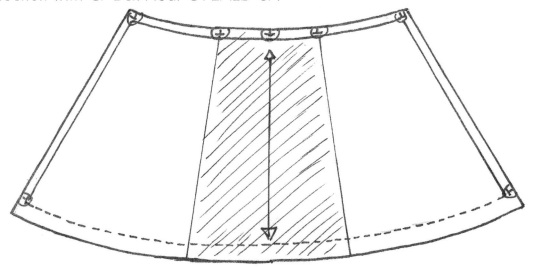

-Skirt section with CF Box Pleat folded to show PLEAT:

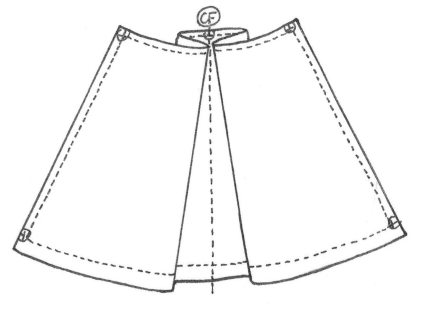

SKIRTS
CIRCLE SKIRT

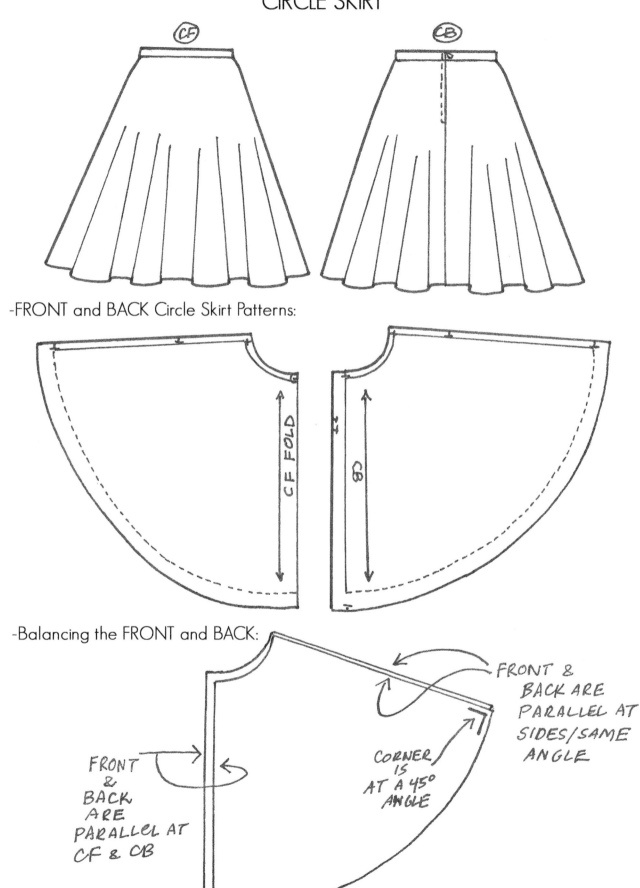

-FRONT and BACK Circle Skirt Patterns:

CF FOLD

CB

-Balancing the FRONT and BACK:

FRONT & BACK ARE PARALLEL AT SIDES/SAME ANGLE

FRONT & BACK ARE PARALLEL AT CF & CB

CORNER IS AT A 45° ANGLE

SKIRTS
CIRCLE SKIRT

WAISTBAND for CIRCLE SKIRT:

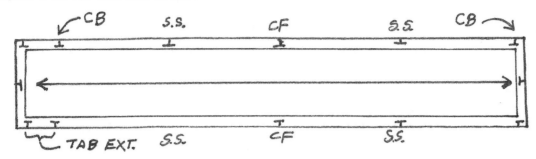

Waistband Interfacing:

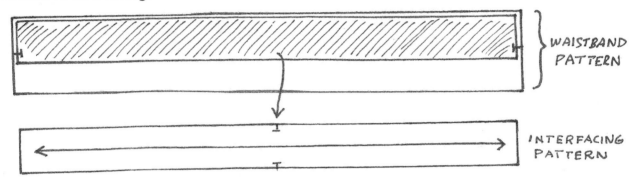

WAISTBAND PATTERN

INTERFACING PATTERN

IN-SEAM POCKETS:

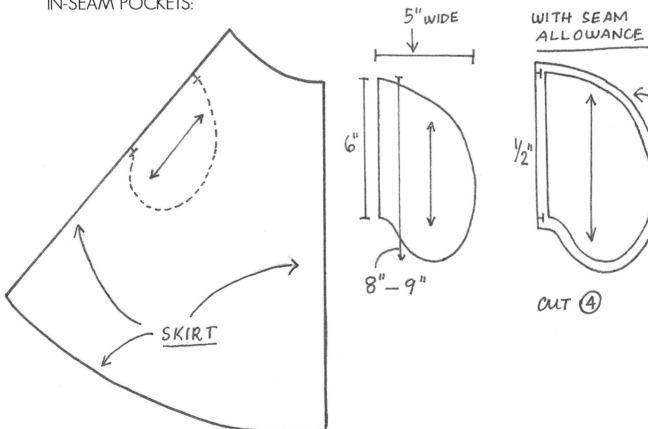

5" WIDE

6"

8" – 9"

WITH SEAM ALLOWANCE

½"

½"

CUT ④

SKIRT

CIRCLE SKIRT w/ WAISTBAND & INSEAM POCKETS
SEWING INSTRUCTIONS

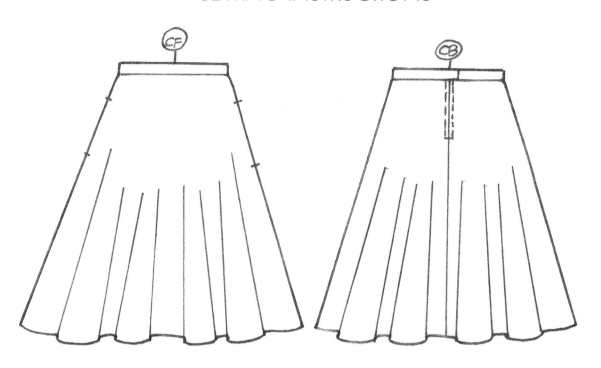

After cutting pieces in muslin, you can begin sewing:

1) Sewing POCKETS and SIDE SEAMS.
   -Take all four pocket pieces/patterns. Position 2 pocket pieces on FRONT of skirt, right sides facing each other. Stitch pocket to front of skirt from TOP pocket notch to BOTTOM pocket notch.

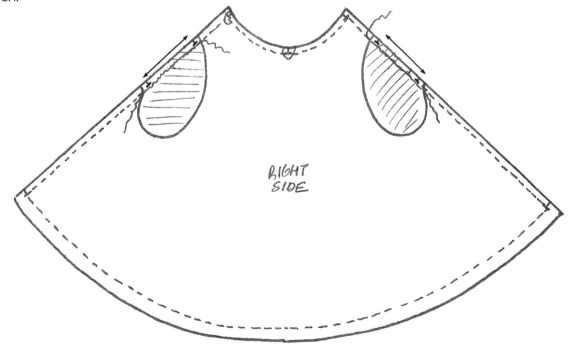

CIRCLE SKIRT w/ WAISTBAND & INSEAM POCKETS
SEWING INSTRUCTIONS

Repeat prior step for the skirt BACK.

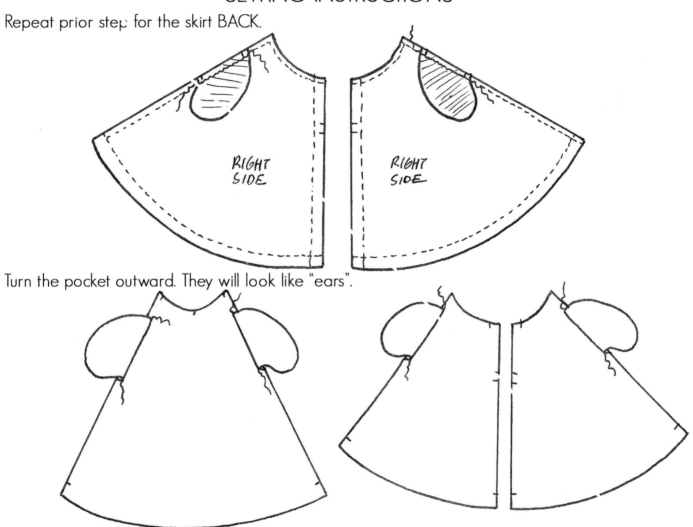

RIGHT SIDE

RIGHT SIDE

Turn the pocket outward. They will look like "ears".

Align the skirt FRONT and BACK, right sides together. Stitch along the side seams at 1/2" seam allowance. Sew from the waistline to the top of the pocket, around the pocket and continue to the hem of the skirt. Press side seams open (except where pockets are)

WRONG SIDES

CIRCLE SKIRT w/ WAISTBAND & INSEAM POCKETS
SEWING INSTRUCTIONS

Turn the skirt right side out. Once you have done this, you can see that the inseam pockets are hidden inside the side seams.

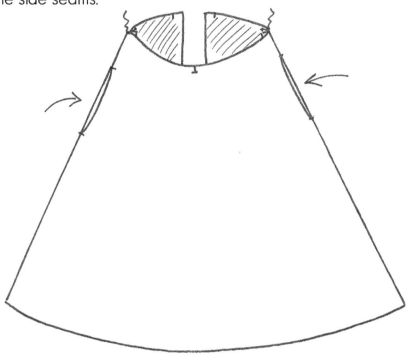

Sew CENTER BACK seam at 1" seam allowance, from zipper double notches to hem of skirt. Leave the center back seam open—approximately 7 ½"-8". This is where you will sew the zipper.

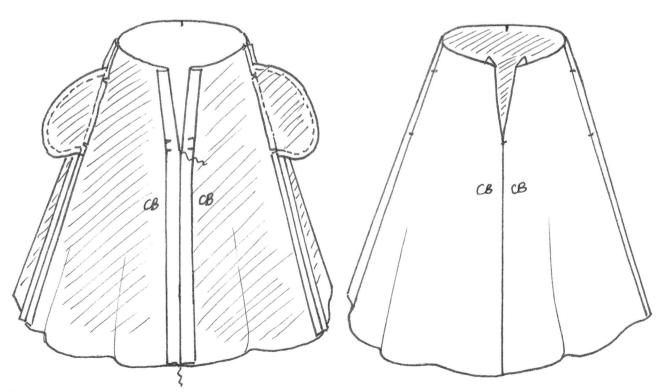

SKIRTS
CIRCLE SKIRT w/ WAISTBAND & INSEAM POCKETS
SEWING INSTRUCTIONS

Sew lapped zipper. Refer to Sewing Textbook for Instructions.

Sew the waistband onto the waist of the skirt. Follow the instructions in the Sewing Textbook on "sewing waistbands" and make sure the waistband extension is on the left side of the back skirt as shown:

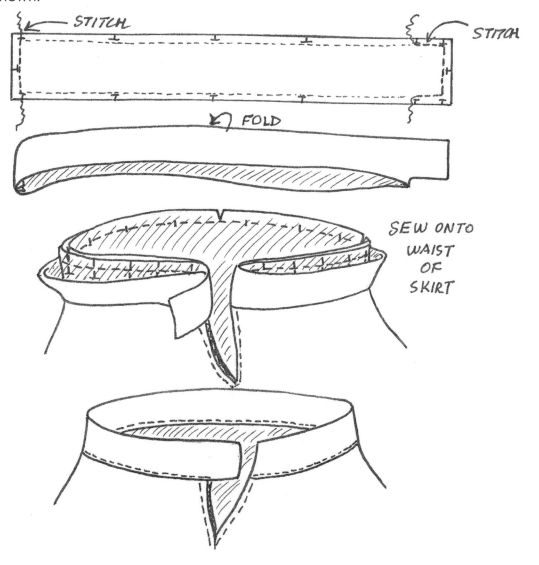

STITCH

STITCH

FOLD

SEW ONTO
WAIST
OF
SKIRT

SLEEVES
PUFF SLEEVE

**Follow Directions as shown in Pattern Drafting Textbook for ALL of the following Sleeves:

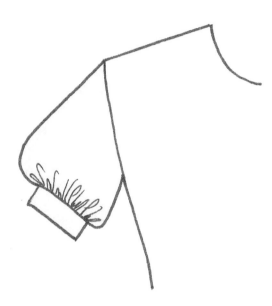

A) Use Dartless Sleeve Block/Sloper
   or Regular Sleeve Block/Sloper

B) Puff Sleeve Pre-Draft

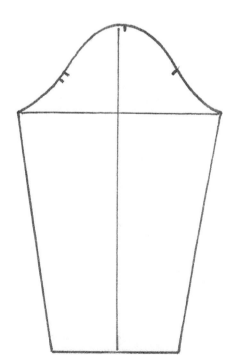

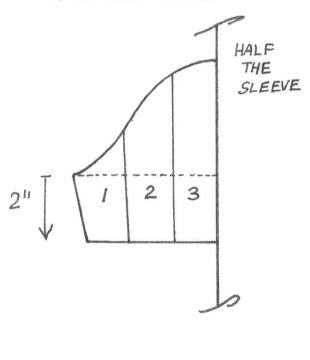

HALF THE SLEEVE

2"

1 2 3

C) Slash & Spread:

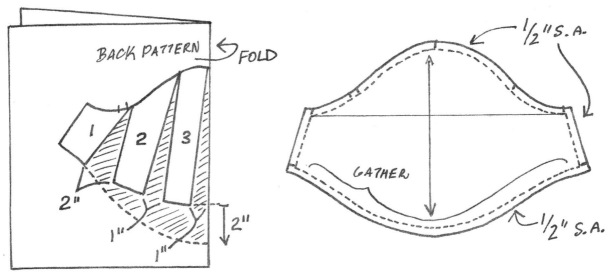

BACK PATTERN ← FOLD

1 2 3

2" 1" 1" 2"

D) Add Seam Allowances:

½" S.A.

GATHER

½" S.A.

E) Sleeve Band/Cuff Draft:

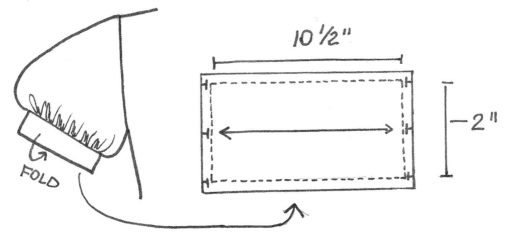

FOLD

10 ½"

2"

F) Sleeve Band/Cuff Interfacing Pattern:

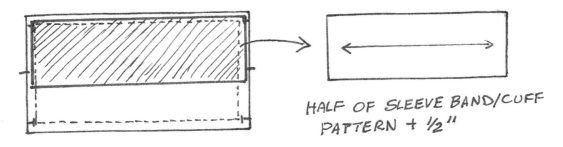

HALF OF SLEEVE BAND/CUFF
PATTERN + ½"

SLEEVES

PUFF SLEEVE: FULLNESS AT CAP

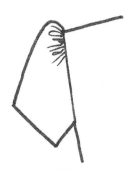

A) Use Dartless Sleeve Block/Sloper or Regular Sleeve Block/Sloper:

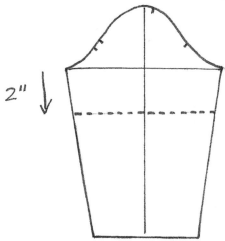

2"

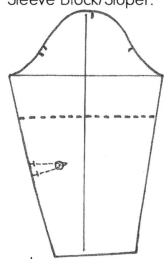

B) Pre-Draft Sleeve:

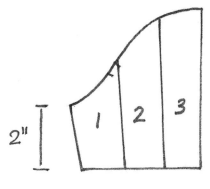

2"

1   2   3

HALF OF SLEEVE.

C) Slash & Spread:

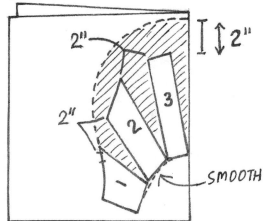

2"

2"

2   3

2"

SMOOTH

D) Add Seam Allowances:

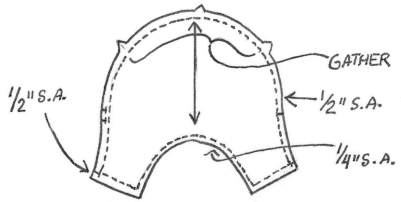

GATHER

1/2" S.A.

1/2" S.A.

1/4" S.A.

SLEEVES
BISHOP SLEEVE

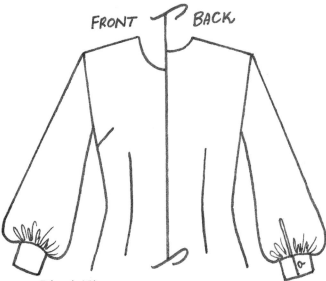

FRONT BACK

A) Use Dartless Sleeve Block/Sloper—
Divide Sleeve into FOUR (4) sections:

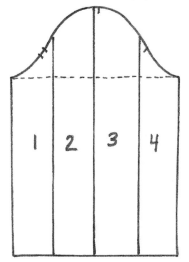

1 2 3 4

B) Drop hem area only at the back of sleeve:

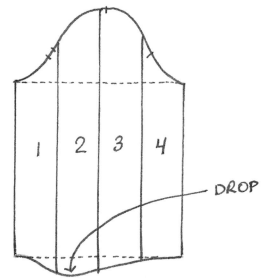

1 2 3 4

DROP

C) Slash & Spread as shown:

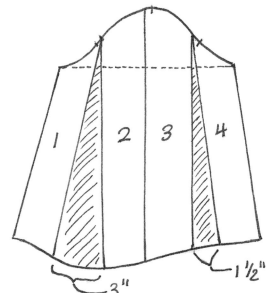

1 2 3 4

3"   1½"

D) Add Slit for Placket at Back Hem area:

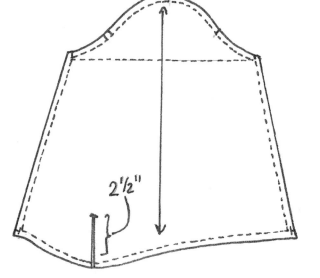

2½"

50.

LEG OF MUTTON SLEEVE

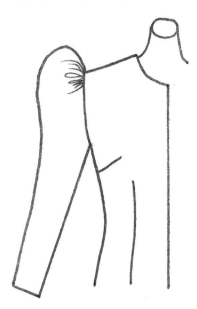

A) Use Dartless Sleeve
   Block/Sloper:

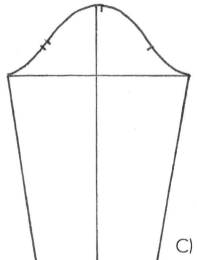

C) Slash & Spread Sleeve:

B) Pre-Draft Sleeve:

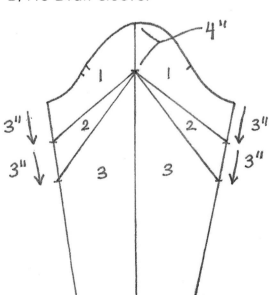

4"

1   1

3"   2   2   3"

3"   3   3   3"

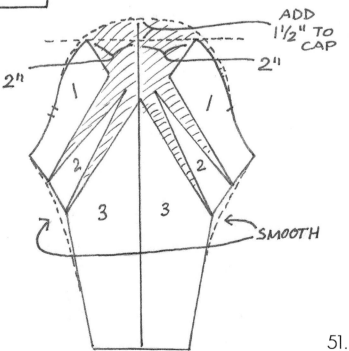

ADD
1½" TO
CAP

2"   2"

1   1

2   2

3   3

SMOOTH

SLEEVES
RAGLAN SLEEVE

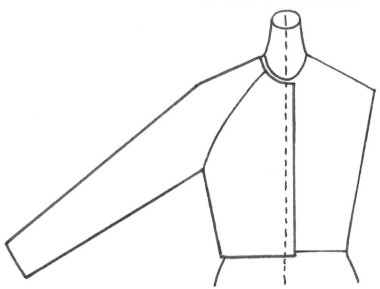

-Use Basic Bodice One Dart Front Block/Sloper and Basic Bodice Back Block/Sloper as well as Basic Sleeve Block/Sloper:

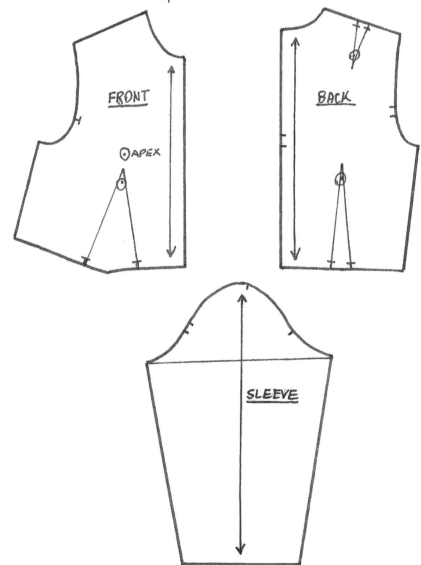

FRONT

⊙APEX

BACK

SLEEVE

SLEEVES
RAGLAN SLEEVE

A) Modify FRONT and BACK Blocks/Slopers as shown:

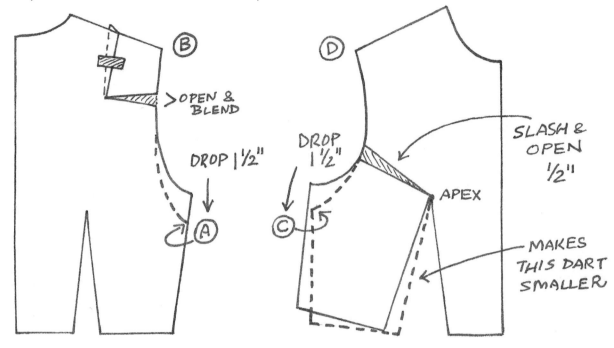

OPEN & BLEND

DROP 1½"

Ⓐ

Ⓑ

Ⓒ

Ⓓ

DROP 1½"

SLASH & OPEN ½"

APEX

MAKES THIS DART SMALLER

B) Back and Front RAGLAN Yoke Draft:

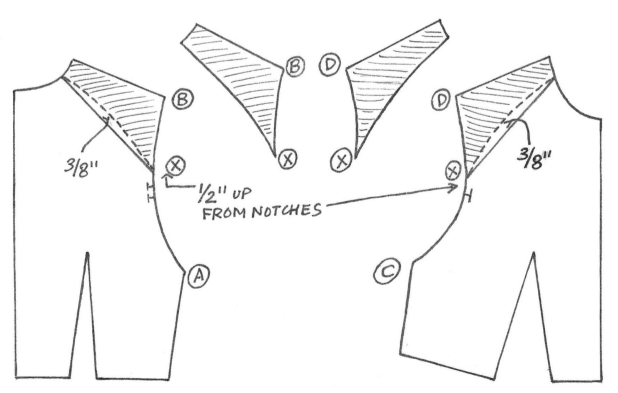

3/8"

Ⓑ

Ⓧ

½" UP FROM NOTCHES

Ⓐ

Ⓑ Ⓓ

Ⓧ Ⓧ

Ⓓ

Ⓧ

3/8"

Ⓒ

RAGLAN SLEEVE

C) Modifying the Sleeve Cap:

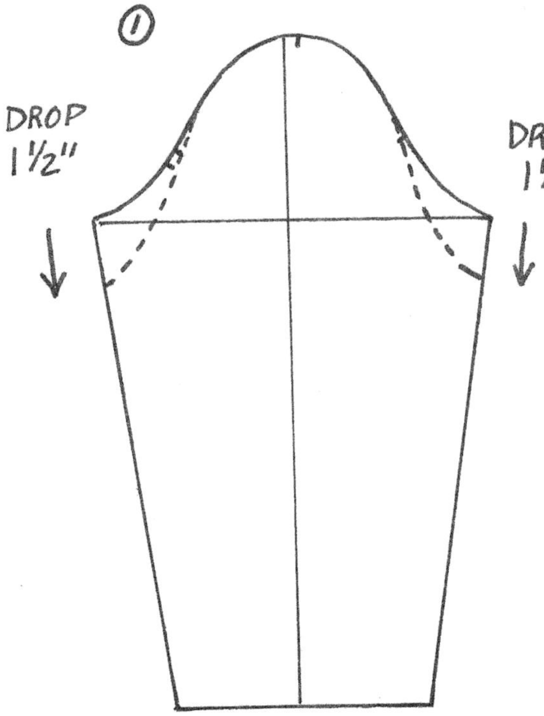

①
DROP 1½"
DROP 1½"

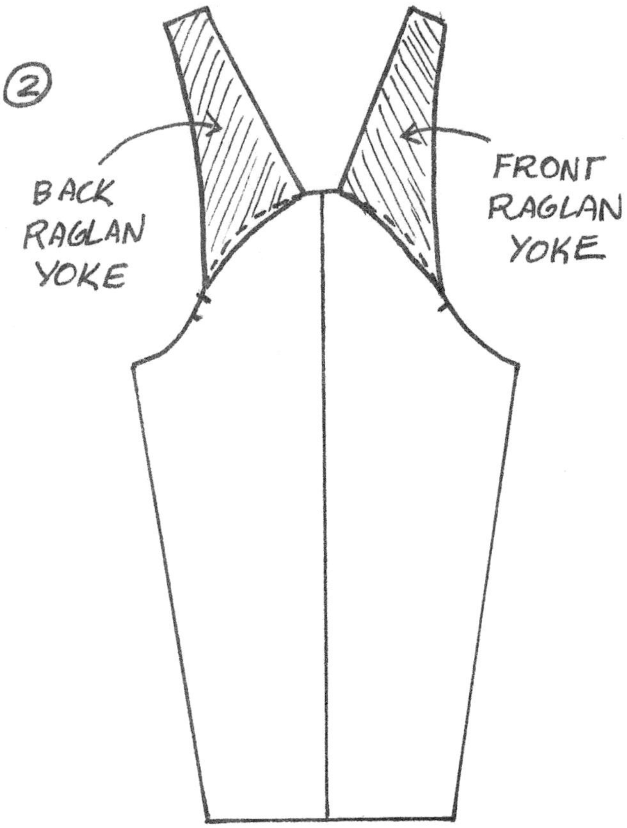

②
BACK RAGLAN YOKE
FRONT RAGLAN YOKE

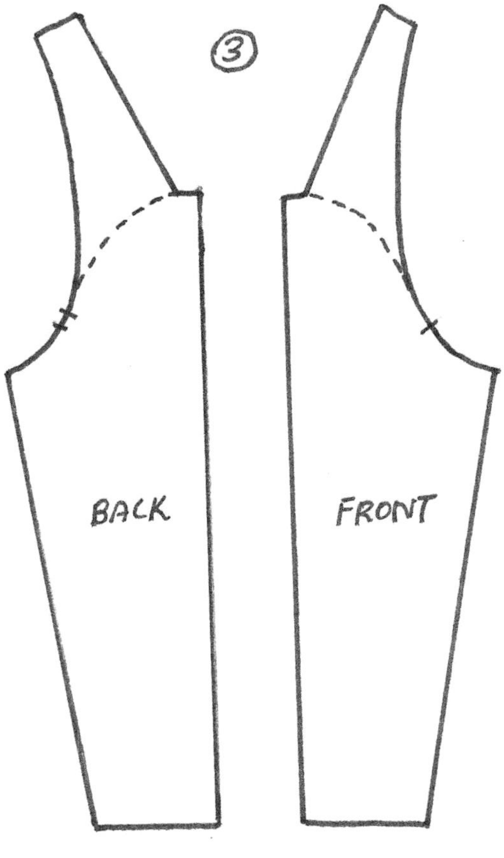

③
BACK
FRONT

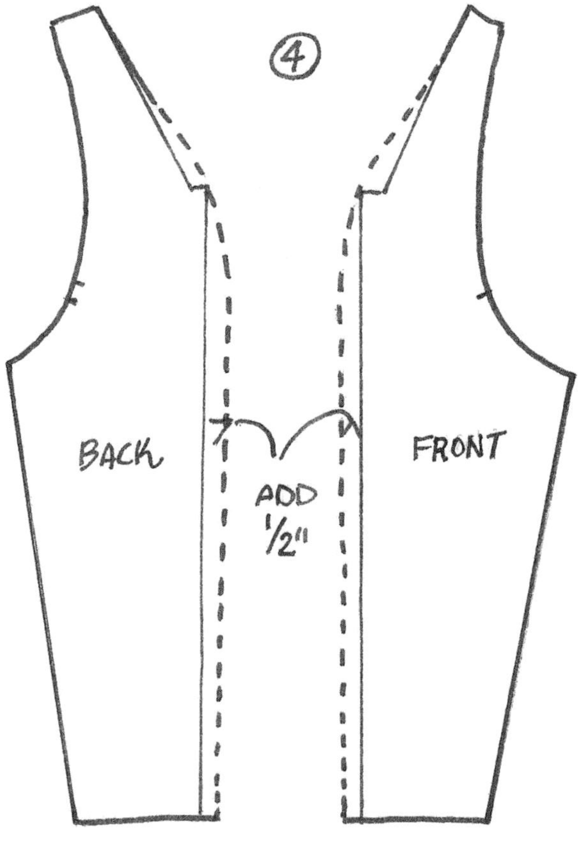

④
BACK
FRONT
ADD ½"

D) Balance FRONT and BACK Raglan Sleeves by putting Front over Back (or visa versa) sections on top of each other and make sure they are parallel:

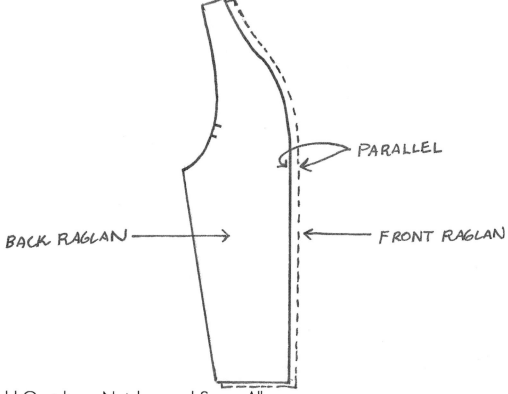

PARALLEL

BACK RAGLAN ⟶

⟵ FRONT RAGLAN

E) Add Grainlines, Notches and Seam Allowances

BACK

FRONT

CAN BE CUT ON THE BIAS

CAN BE CUT ON THE BIAS

FRONT

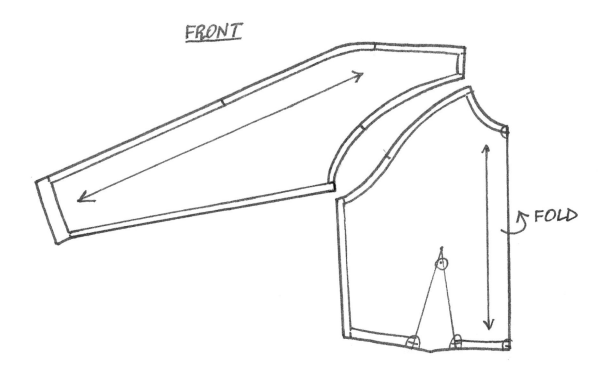

FOLD

BACK

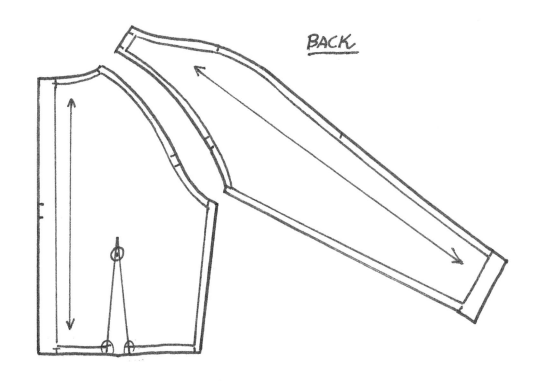

SLEEVES
KIMONO SLEEVE

Follow Directions as shown in Pattern Drafting Textbook for ALL of the following Sleeves

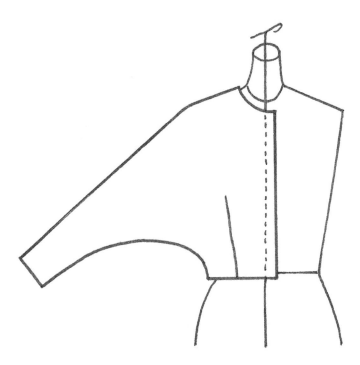

-To Draft Kimono Sleeve, use Basic Bodice One Dart Front Block/Sloper and Basic Bodice Back Block/Sloper:

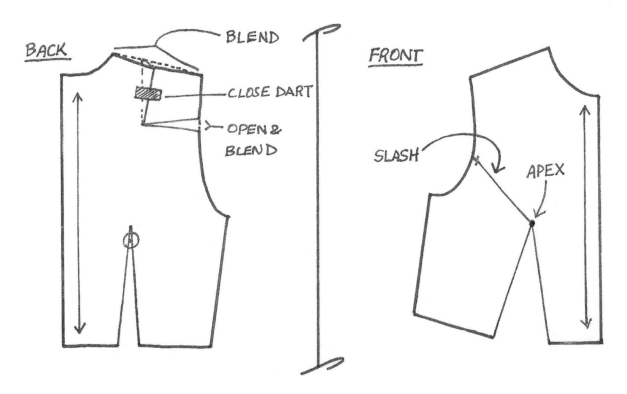

BACK

BLEND

CLOSE DART

OPEN & BLEND

FRONT

SLASH

APEX

SLEEVES
KIMONO SLEEVE

A) Begin drafting Kimono Sleeve by creating the BACK pattern:

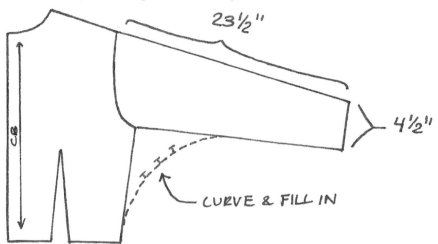

23½"

4½"

CB

CURVE & FILL IN

B) Trace and...

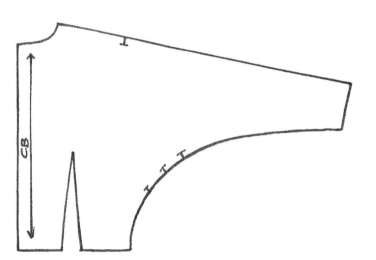

CB

C) Follow directions in Pattern Drafting Textbook for FRONT:

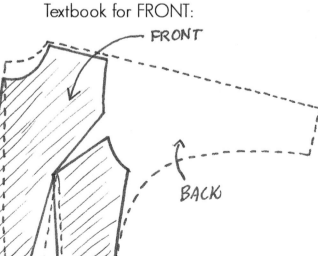

FRONT

BACK

D) Balance FRONT & BACK patterns:

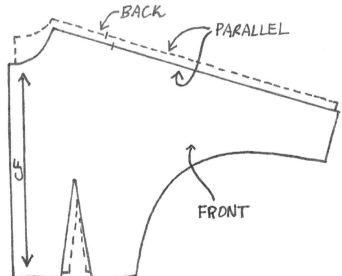

BACK

PARALLEL

CF

FRONT

58.

DRESSES
EXAMPLES FOR
FINAL PROJECT

DRESSES USING
ALL SKILLS LEARNED
IN ASSIGNMENTS:
COLLARS
DART MANIPULATION
SKIRT
SLEEVES

DRESSES

EXAMPLES FOR FINAL PROJECT

DRESSES USING
ALL SKILLS LEARNED
IN ASSIGNMENTS:
COLLARS
DART MANIPULATION
SKIRT
SLEEVES

60.

Printed in Great Britain
by Amazon